Return to Wake Robin

The memories float back to me
In the cool scent of water on the breeze
In the shadows and sifting sunlight on the lake bottom sand
In the sound of the waves as they softly kiss the shore
In the rhythmic ping of a sailboat's bobbing
In the whisper of the wind through the pines
In the call of a loon's lonely lyrics
In the white, sunlit feathers of an eagle's flight

These are those memories . . .

Return to Wake Robin

One Cabin in the Heyday of Northwoods Resorts

Marnie O. Mamminga

Wisconsin Historical Society Press

Published by the Wisconsin Historical Society Press

Publishers since 1855

© 2012 by Marnie O. Mamminga

wisconsin**history**.org

All photos are from the Oatman family collection unless otherwise indicated.

ADDITIONAL PHOTOS:
Page iii, the author enjoying a quiet moment, with writing pad and pencil, during her birthday picnic at No-Pi-Ming, circa 1955; pages v, 20, and 39: trillium illustration, from *Dictionary of Gardening*, vol. 4, 1951; page vii, Moody's Camp, circa 1920s and '30s: a fleet of wooden rowboats used for fishing or pleasure waits at the camp's boat dock along the north shore of Big Spider Lake; page viii, Spider Chain of Lakes map, 1965, courtesy of Dick Seitz; page 185, the author and her mother, circa 1955; page 186, the author, 2011.

Printed in Wisconsin, U.S.A.

16 15 14 13 12   2 3 4 5

Library of Congress Cataloging-in-Publication Data

Mamminga, Marnie O.

  Return to Wake Robin : one cabin in the heyday of Northwoods Resorts / Marnie O. Mamminga.

    p. cm.

  ISBN 978-0-87020-491-3 (hardcover : alk. paper) 1. Camps—Wisconsin—History. 2. Resorts—Wisconsin—History. I. Title.

  GV194.W6M35 2012

  796.5409775—dc23

                    2011030177

To

My sons
John, Bob, and Tom
For sharing their kind and joyful spirits

My daughters-in-law
Lara and Jennifer
For embracing the lake, the cabin, and us

My grandchildren
Lily, Amber, Joy, Elena, Ryan, and those to come . . .
That their happy hearts might know the story

But especially
To Dave
Sweetheart, buddy, husband—
For believing in me

Contents

×

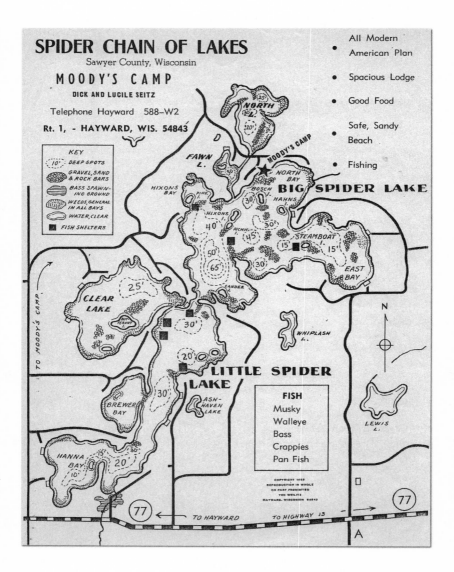

SPIDER CHAIN OF LAKES

Sawyer County, Wisconsin

MOODY'S CAMP

DICK AND LUCILE SEITZ

Telephone Hayward   588—W2

Rt. 1, - HAYWARD, WIS. 54843

- All Modern American Plan
- Spacious Lodge
- Good Food
- Safe, Sandy Beach
- Fishing

KEY

- 10' — DEEP SPOTS
- GRAVEL, SAND & ROCK BARS
- BASS SPAWNING GROUND
- WEEDS, GENERAL IN ALL BAYS
- WATER, CLEAR
- FISH SHELTERS

NORTH L.

FAWN L.

MOODY'S CAMP

NORTH BAY

BIG SPIDER LAKE

HIXONS BAY

PINE

BOSCH

HAHNS

HIXONS

PICNIC

STEAMBOAT

SANDER L.

EAST BAY

CLEAR LAKE

BUTTERNUT L.

WHIPLASH L.

LITTLE SPIDER LAKE

BREWER BAY

ASH-HAVEN LAKE

LEWIS L.

FISH

Musky
Walleye
Bass
Crappies
Pan Fish

HANNA BAY

N

COPYRIGHT 1962
REPRODUCTION IN WHOLE
OR PART PROHIBITED
TED WEILITZ
HAYWARD, WISCONSIN 54843

77

TO HAYWARD

TO HIGHWAY 13

77

A

Preface

The log cabins are disappearing.

The camps are nearly gone as well. Like the early morning mist slowly vaporizing on the water, so, too, have vanished the ribbed wooden rowboats, the sound of squeaking oar locks, the red-and-white bobbers bobbing off lines at sunset, the call of square dances, the warm glow of kerosene lanterns, the putzing purr of 3-horsepower motors, the ring of the lodge bell, the combined laughter of chore boys and cabin girls.

The remaining relics symbolic of this era, these quaint log cabins are swiftly being replaced by large, suburban-style homes along the shorelines of Northwoods lakes. Sadly, with these teardowns a valuable history of a time, place, and culture is vanishing.

Return to Wake Robin is a series of vignettes reflecting on the golden years of Northwoods resorts through the history of one camp and cabin from the 1920s through the 1960s: my family's 1929 log cabin, Wake Robin, and the former neighboring resort, Moody's Camp, both located on Big Spider Lake—part of a chain of five lakes connected by beguiling thoroughfares—near Hayward, Wisconsin. This time frame represents the historical high point of camps and cabins, sandwiched between the turn-of-the-last-century logging era and the 1970s right-angle turn toward modernized lake homes, condo associations, and Jet Skis.

By all accounts, the 1920s through 1960s was a time vacationers went to the woods because it was *different* from home and offered a change from the urban lifestyle. Through these more primitive log camps and cabins, life became freer and less restrictive. These retreats were the essence of simplicity. Like Thoreau, all one needed were the basics and a boat.

Covering a broad range of topics, these essays focus on

A vintage postcard offers an aerial view of Big Spider and its connecting chain of lakes.

representative elements of life in the Northwoods: the fishing guides, resort owners, square dances, camp and cabin activities. They follow a chronological pattern from the beginning of Moody's Camp in the 1920s to the late 1960s, when the second owners, the Seitzes, sold the resort and the camp community basically ended. A collection of vintage photos provides visual documentation of this world.

The people and events I chose to highlight in *Return to Wake Robin* are representative of the interwoven history shared by Wake Robin and Moody's Camp. Founded in the early 1920s by Ted Moody, a local legend and early Northwoods entrepreneur, Moody's Camp was a destination for many Midwesterners seeking the clear air, pristine water, and rejuvenating beauty of the Northwoods. The juxtaposition of the camp's rustic simplicity with its elegant charms lured a host of eager vacationers to the resort's stunning shoreline, great fishing, and scrumptious meals graciously served three times a day.

My grandparents, Erle and Clara Oatman, like many of the 1920s era, were two of those from Illinois who were smitten with their initial discovery of the Northwoods and all that it had to offer. Having chanced upon Moody's Camp around 1924 while vacationing nearby, they soon started spending summer vacations there. It didn't take them long to fall in love with the lake and develop a close friendship with Ted and Myrtle Moody. And so, in

The main lodge of Moody's Camp with its charming garden, circa 1930s, was a gathering place for guests as well as neighbors.

MAIN LODGE   MOODY'S CAMP ON BIG SPIDER LAKE, HAYWARD, WIS. 33

a move to put down permanent roots, my grandparents decided to construct their own log cabin on the first available land next door to the resort.

In 1929 Wake Robin was built. Christened after the common name for the wildflower trillium that carpets the surrounding woodland from May to early June, its simple log-cabin charms and screened porch have now been enjoyed by five generations. Eighty-three years later little has changed. Today it stands as one of the last remnants on Big Spider Lake representing that period of Northwoods history.

To write these essays, I drew from my sixty-two years of memories and observations of life on the lake. I also interviewed those I grew up with who lived this era and helped shape my memories, including a former fishing guide, one of the resort's owners, and my family and friends. Special gratitude goes out to: my parents, Dave and Woody Oatman, for their fine love of history and storytelling; my siblings, Nancy, David, Tom, and Mary, for their perseverance and grace on our life journey together, and for sharing the Oatman shoebox archives; my husband, Dave, for his devoted appreciation of the Northwoods and for serving as enthusiastic first reader of my manuscript; my sons John, Bob, and Tom and my daughters-in-law Lara and Jennifer for their continual interest and encouragement; Dick Seitz and the entire Seitz family for photos and details; Franklin and Vera Hobart for their wonderful

This circa 1929 photo shows Wake Robin shortly after it was completed. My father helped gather the rocks for the fieldstone fireplace, which were then individually hand chiseled by a local mason. The tamarack logs were also hand hewed and chinked, with the cornices staggered in length.

Northwoods album; and lifelong lake friends—the Mraz, Perrine, Hines, Halfvarson, Seehuetter, Wahl, and Wedding families—for their delightful reminiscing over the years. Grateful appreciation also goes out to the entire staff at the Wisconsin Historical Society Press, especially Kate Thompson and my excellent editor Laura Kearney.

Collectively, these remembrances and photos symbolize a culture in the heyday of its charms. In writing these vignettes, I sought not only to offer a prototype of a vanishing time and place but to speak to the depth of spirit, beloved by many, that emanated from the Northwoods during this period. My hope is that *Return to Wake Robin* will ring true for all those who lived this era and also offer a glimpse of a treasured time for those who did not.

—*Marnie Oatman Mamminga*

Prologue

Sleek and silent, he sailed through the morning mist. Only the whir of his wings whispered through the still air above the shadowed, sleeping forest. His elegant, powerful body rode the rosy rays of a rising sunrise like a swift spirit sent from heaven. His journey had been long and arduous, but he knew where he was headed. He pushed onward.

Suddenly, he sensed he was almost there. The song of his soul joyfully broke the cool quiet in an undulating wave of ancient melody. He circled only once, then floated down through the silver mist to the water below. Spotting the islands he was looking for, he stretched his wings, banked to the left and with effortless ease glided onto the still lake, leaving just a hint of a rippled wake.

In a sweet lyrical hymn, the loon sang out his welcoming call. Across the bay, another echoed his greeting.

A loon on
Big Spider Lake

Passing the Torch

*"This grand show is eternal. It is always sunrise somewhere;
the dew is never all dried at once; a shower is forever falling; vapor
ever rising. Eternal sunrise, eternal sunset, eternal dawn and
gloaming . . . each in its turn, as the round earth rolls."*
—John Muir

Summer 1964, a Northwoods Lake

"Get up! Get up!" my mother whispers.

My eyes flash open. Confusion clouds my brain. Where am I? Is something wrong? I quickly look around.

I'm sandwiched between frayed woolen blankets and the sagging mattress of an old metal bed on the porch of our family log cabin. Looking almost exactly as it did when my grandparents built it in 1929, it sits high on a hill surrounded by the pine-and-musty fragrance of the woods.

Through sleepy eyelids I take in the green porch swing, the birch-legged table, and the smoky glass of the kerosene lantern reflecting the stillness of the lake below.

Having escaped the steamy cornland of my home for a few summer weeks, I believe I'm in heaven on earth. My face luxuriates in the coolness of the early morning air. I relax and curl deeper beneath the blankets' warmth.

"Get up!" my mother's voice whispers again. "You must come now. The sunrise is simply glorious!"

The sunrise? Get up to see the sunrise? Who's she kidding? The last thing this fourteen-year-old wants to do is leave a warm bed to go see a sunrise, glorious or otherwise. It's 5:00 a.m. and it's freezing out there.

"Hurry!" my mother urges.

Being careful not to let the screen door slam, she sets off down the forty-nine log steps at a determined rate of speed to the lake below.

In the twin bed opposite me, my seventeen-year-old sister Nancy stirs. She pushes back the covers and plops to the floor. Not to be outdone, I make a supreme effort and struggle out of bed as well. In our thin cotton nighties, we grab our father's World War II pea-green army blankets from the ends of our beds and wrap them tightly around our shoulders.

As our bare feet touch the cold porch floor, we are thunderbolted awake. Our pace quickens. One of us misses catching the screen door. It slams. Like a couple of water bugs hopscotching across the lake to avoid fish jaws, we gingerly pick our way over slippery rocks and prickly pine needles down the forty-nine dew-covered log steps to the shore.

When we feel we've saved our feet from any horny toads or big black spiders that might be crazy enough to be up this early, we catch our breath and look up. Our mother's silhouette is outlined against a golden dawn, the first light catching the soft red of her hair. She is right. It is a glorious sunrise.

Across the lake a sliver of the most splendid red crests the top of the shadowed forest. Hues of lavender, rose, and amber begin to pulsate into the sky like a kaleidoscope. High above in the pale blueness, a lone star still sparkles. Silver mist rises gently from the smoothness of the lake. All is still. In the sacred silence, my mother, sister, and I stand reverently together against a backdrop of tall pine and watch the magic of dawn unfold.

Suddenly the curve of a brilliant sun bursts through the dark forest. The world begins to awaken. We watch a blue heron lift up from a distant shore and gently fan its way over the still waters. Two ducks make a rippled landing near our dock while a black-and-white beauty—a loon—skims along the edge of a nearby island hunting for its morning meal.

Breathing in the chill air, the three of us draw our blankets closer. The gentle hues of the sunrise turn into the brightness of a new day and the last star fades. My sister and I take one more look, race up the steps, and jump into our beds to grab a few more hours of sleep.

My mother is more reluctant to leave the sunrise's amphitheater.

From the renewed warmth of my bed, it is a while longer before I hear her reach the top step and gently close the porch door.

Summer 1994, a Northwoods Lake

"Get up! Get up!" I whisper to my adolescent sons sleeping dreamily in the same old metal beds of our family cabin's porch.

"Come see the sunrise! It's awesome!"

Wake Robin's porch screen door, bathed in the warm light of an early morning sunrise, late 1990s

Amazingly, I watch as my fourth-generation cabin snoozers rouse themselves from their slumber. They snatch the World War II pea-green army blankets from the ends of their beds and stumble out the porch door. It slams. Gingerly they maneuver slippery rocks and prickly pine needles down forty-nine dew-covered log steps to the lakeshore.

Their seventy-four-year-old grandmother is already there. Her red hair, now streaked with white, reflects the first light.

She greets her grandsons with a quiet smile, gathers her blanket closer, and turns toward the east to observe once again the magic of dawn unfold.

My sons' faces watch intently as the rich colors of the sunrise soar into the sky like the radiant plumage of a mystical bird. It isn't long before the flap of a blue heron's wing and the melodic call of a loon awaken the lake with activity.

"Isn't it beautiful?" I whisper.

The boys nod in silent agreement. Their grandmother smiles at them. Before long, they grab the tails of their frayed blankets and race back up the steps to the welcome coziness of their beds.

My mother and I stay a little longer. Standing close, we watch the swirls of pearl mist rise and the sky bloom into the shades of a morning rose. We are rewarded this day by the graceful glide of an eagle high overhead. The gentle rays of the early sun warm our faces.

Eventually, we turn to begin our slow climb up the old log stairs. Half way up I catch my breath and look back to see how my mother is doing. But she is not there. She has changed her mind. Through the treetops I can see her, still on the lakeshore, lingering in the light.

Ted and Myrtle Moody Create Their Camp

1922–1955

"Here there is no time."

Ted Moody was a presence.

Whether it was his size or his personality, you always knew when he was around. And over the years, that presence evolved into a legend.

Like the black bears that roam the northern woods of Wisconsin, Ted's tall stature and ample girth were impressive. The charismatic Swede also had charm—and the humor to match.

As the founder of Moody's Camp, established in 1922–1923, he figures largely into the development of Big Spider Lake's north shore, the surrounding private cabins, local tourism, and the sport of fishing. Along with his lovely wife, Myrtle, the two offered their clients as delightful and gracious a resort as anywhere in the Northwoods.

Due to health problems caused by breathing in car fumes while working as an in-demand mechanic in an Elgin, Illinois, auto garage, Ted was told he didn't have long to live. (He enjoyed a tall tale, and this might be one of them. It's peppered with the drama that Ted loved.)

But never say die to a Swede. Slamming the door on death's knock, Ted and Myrtle stepped on the gas and hightailed it up to the crisp, pure air of the Northwoods to start a new life. Scouting for property in the Sawyer County lakes region near Hayward, Wisconsin, they eventually came across the pristine, quiet beauty of Big Spider Lake.

Despite no formal training in resort management, Ted instinctively knew the realtor's mantra: location, location, location.

He couldn't have chosen better.

Setting his camp on a high ridge at the north end of the lake, Ted utilized its magnificent, sweeping vistas; its scattering of majestic islands; its grand moon rise on the opposite shore; its glorious sunrises; its clear, clean waters for fishing, boating, or

The view of the islands from Moody's Camp, circa 1920s, was one of the loveliest on the lake.

swimming; and its sparkling views of the Milky Way, constellations, shooting stars, and the northern lights.

With the vision of a great winged owl, Ted wisely honed in on one of the choicest spots in the area. Bequeathed with a showman's personality, however, Ted was not about to let Mother Nature steal the whole show.

With a keen sense of entrepreneurship, Ted put a creative spin on the term "fishing camp." Instead of the usual rough and rustic lodgings, Ted and Myrtle's camp had elegance and class.

To their guests, "Welcome to the Northwoods" meant dining room tables covered with starched, white linen cloths set with fine china and silverware and topped with vases of sunny wildflowers; a hand-hewn log lodge decorated with great boughs of fresh, fragrant pine; a sitting room with a baby grand piano; a welcoming roaring fire in a stately fieldstone fireplace; and a host of friendly help who served and catered to every need.

The Moody's Camp dining room, circa 1935: decorated with white table-cloths, wildflower bouquets, and pine boughs every night for dinner

Franklin and Vera Hobart Collection

Ted was a master mechanic, but he could also boast of his building skills, and along with his well designed, spacious lodge, he constructed thirteen cozy log cabins for his guests—each cleaned and tidied daily by cabin girls, warmed by wood-burning stoves, and serviced by chore boys, who, with a ring of the lodge's cast-iron bell, came running to answer any guest's latest need. Most of the cabins had spectacular lake views, and a few even sported screened porches cooled by pine-scented breezes.

There was no rustic grub in this camp. Guests were served three sumptuous meals a day with rotating nightly menus that included prime rib, T-bone steaks, lobster, and, on Sunday, a Swedish smorgasbord laden with an endless array of delectable homemade dishes. Fresh pies, wild woodland berries, and locally harvested maple syrup–topped sundaes concluded the feasts.

Toss in an assortment of enticing, organized activities that included picnics, nature hikes, and square dances—all of which simply required the guests to show up—and Ted and Myrtle had one hell of a "fishing camp."

It's no wonder the Moodys instantly built up a strong and loyal following. Although they printed alluring brochures, word of their gracious hospitality, entwined with lake and forest fun-filled activities, spread faster than a marketer's advertising dream.

It wasn't long before guests began returning year after year. Some liked the place so much, they decided to stay, and soon private summer cabins began to ring either side of the resort. Erle and Clara Oatman, my grandparents, were two of the first to do so.

A vintage postcard of the lodge at Moody's Camp shows the original building before the living area was added.

Franklin and Vera Hobart Collection

Great fishing, of course, was a given. With excellent guides, a well-stocked bait house, and boats at the ready, those who came to fish were almost always guaranteed success. For those who sought other Northwoods pleasures, Ted had a few ideas up his sleeve.

Like a well-oiled rifle, he shot out enough amusing adventures to capture even the slickest of city slickers. Besides the renowned weekly square dances, there were festive lodge costume parties; hikes under the sun-dappled branches of a nearby, still-standing virgin forest; trips to the cascading amber waters of Copper Falls; and picnics on enchanting, breeze-swept islands. Guests could choose from all of the above or just laze by the lake. When all met up for the evening meal, the lodge was a cacophony of shared tales.

Ted also possessed a certain flair for the mischievous and loved a good practical joke. Although the male and female guests always dressed up for dinner—the ladies in floral silk dresses and the men in khakis and Pendleton shirts—newly arrived gentlemen, not aware of Ted's traditions, often showed up sporting ties.

With much ado, Ted would welcome the erring gent in front of all, and then with a flourish would whip out a hefty pair of scissors and promptly cut off his tie. The newcomer was duly embarrassed, and the dining room rocked with delighted laughter.

You had to be a good sport to be around Ted because sometimes his antics were not so hilarious. With the tiny newlywed cabin built for some odd reason just yards away from the lodge, newlyweds were frequent targets of his "jokes." Needless to say, they did not always laugh.

In addition, he liked to flirt with the ladies. With a twinkle in his eye, he was known to greet them by intoning: "I bow to the fourth button." The ladies were charmed. Little children were equally surprised when he scooped them up into great bear hugs. With his large and domineering personality, you never quite knew what Ted would do next.

The Wednesday night T-bone steak fries, however, were his pride and joy—and an unchanging tradition. After all had been served, Ted would stride into the dining room in his tall white chef's hat and apron and ask in his booming voice, "Izz it gooooot?"

"Noooooo!" the guests shouted back, a sure indication that the meal was a huge success.

Myrtle was Ted's opposite, not only in stature but in temperament. Next to his imposing frame, she was as petite as a fawn. Possessed of a refined and quiet nature, Myrtle balanced Ted's exuberance. Besides her fine cooking, especially her homemade desserts, she was an accomplished gardener. The first thing that greeted guests when they finally arrived at the lodge's entrance was the sight of her circular, fieldstone-rimmed garden bursting with a blaze of beautiful blooms; purple phlox, golden black-eyed Susans, white daisies, and orange Turk's-cap lilies were the mainstays.

For some reason, her garden was also home to a sturdy log pole from which hung a well-worn fish scale and hook waiting ominously for the next large monster from the deep. When a big fish did make its appearance, which was frequently, the lodge bell rang excitedly to announce the catch. At the very least, Myrtle's garden provided an enchanting backdrop for all the fish photos and most likely softened the fishy fragrance with the perfume of posies.

Although their roles as resort hosts involved long hours and arduous work, both Ted and Myrtle always dressed as if they were

Ted and Myrtle
Moody in front of
Myrtle's camp gar-
den, circa 1938

*Franklin and Vera
Hobart Collection*

about to join the party. In the early years, Ted attired himself in the
fashion of the day: knickers, wool plaid shirts, and leather high-top
boots. Myrtle greeted her guests in pretty voile dresses accented
with sunny aprons and sturdy, white-heeled shoes. One would
never know she was the kitchen supervisor and often the cook.

Perhaps because he chose to defy death early on and start a fishing
camp enterprise, Ted prominently hung a sign in the lodge's dining room that read: "Here there is no time."

And it was true.

One only needed to get up with the sun to know when to
fish; listen for the resonating ring of the cast-iron bell to know
when to show up for meals; choose whatever activity suited the
moment; and fall asleep when the moon rose and stars covered
the heavens.

For most of the citified guests, their real lives back home raced
from one responsibility to another, but here in this Northwoods
paradise—at least for a few special weeks—time stood still.

It was only when the big bell rang its low, mournful farewell and guests piled into their cars and swung around the curve of the dusty gravel lane to head back home that they realized time had somehow marched on. And in that moment, they hung on a hope and a prayer that time would be kind and return them soon for another glorious summer.

Understanding this, Ted and Myrtle made time count. They helped their guests relish each and every precious moment that the Northwoods had to offer. It's not surprising that they energetically operated their resort for thirty-three successful years, leaving competitors back at the campfire.

Finally, however, it became Ted and Myrtle's turn to retire, and they sold the resort in 1955. The Moodys chose sunny Florida for their wintering grounds. It always seemed odd to picture the towering lumberjack Swede in the land of sun and seashells, but by all accounts they loved it there. It was a time to rest.

For many years after, however, the Moodys returned each summer to the cabin Ted built just outside the camp's entrance. There he could keep an eye on all who crossed over the thoroughfare bridge and under the "Ted Moody's Camp" sign. In addition, it was the perfect spot for annual guests and private-cabin owners, many of whom had become lifelong friends, to stop by to visit.

The camp's entrance sign was a welcoming sight for many over the years.

Courtesy of Dick Seitz

Ironically, when Ted died in 1968, his beloved "Ted Moody's Camp" sign, which still hung over the entrance to the resort road, blew down in a magnificent storm. Death had finally caught up to Ted. But like a wily musky avoiding the bait, Ted had outsmarted him long enough to make dreams come true—not only his and Myrtle's, but for the many guests who visited.

For those who lived it, it was a time to keep.

Erle T. Oatman Rediscovers an Old Friend

1922–1938

"The brightest star in the Milky Way"

He loved all things beautiful.

So in 1922, when he stepped out of his open-air Buick after an arduous, two-day drive, he brushed off his long duster coat and announced to all within earshot, "This is God's country!"

And he was right. It was a phrase my grandfather would repeat frequently over his many trips to Sawyer County, such was the beauty that greeted him.

For a man whose dairy-business slogan was "The brightest star in the Milky Way," Erle T. Oatman knew what he was talking about. He had a keen eye for the exquisiteness of nature and an affinity for the spiritual splendor it had to offer: peace, joy, fun, solitude, friendships, awe, and wonder.

Breathing in deeply the fragrant, cool, clean air of the wind, water, and woodlands, he discovered that a love and respect for this heaven of forested lakes grew in him, a sentiment that has flowed like a river down through five generations.

His introduction to the area came, as it did for many, by way of stress. In 1912, Erle and his younger brother William were partners in a family dairy business in Dundee, Illinois, specializing in condensed milk. When World War I came along, the demand for their product skyrocketed to meet the needs of the American troops overseas. Business boomed.

In 1918, after the war ended, the entrepreneurial brothers decided to expand the business, establishing a milk distribution plant at the south end of the Fox River Valley in Aurora, Illinois. William asked Erle to serve as president and head up their new operation: Oatman Brothers Inc.

Shortly after these business transactions occurred, however, William unexpectedly died. Erle faced the daunting challenge of carrying on a new business in a new location with new partners while mourning the loss of his brother.

The solace of the Northwoods beckoned. He answered.

Gathering together a few of his business associates, Erle decided to take a fishing hiatus to the Hayward lakes region in the fall of 1922. As a neophyte to the wilderness, however, Erle needed the appropriate gear and attire, and so, before setting off, he headed into neighboring Chicago to stock up on camp essentials.

Not a man to scrimp, he selected one of Chicago's finest department stores and outfitted himself in a complete fishing wardrobe that included the sportsmen's fashions of the day: wool knickers; long, sturdy stockings; Pendleton shirts; and an all-purpose overcoat and cap that would come in particularly handy to ward off the dust and dirt during the rugged two-day drive in an open car. He also picked up the best of rods, reels, and lures.

He was ready, and he was dapper.

The group of friends chose Boulder Lodge near Clam Lake, run by the Scheer brothers, as their destination. They were not disappointed. After several invigorating weeks of Northwoods scenery and adventures, they returned home refreshed and renewed, bringing with them an abundance of hilarious fish tales and the desire to come back again.

As he was not a selfish man, Erle's first impulse was to share such loveliness with his wife, Clara, and their adored young son, David, my father. Known as a generous and sensitive man, Erle knew his little family would be thrilled by the opportunity to enjoy such an appealing environment. The following summer, the closely knit trio made the trip.

They never looked back.

Returning to Boulder Lodge for several summers thereafter, they relished weeks of fishing, hiking, and exploring the area. One day, as they motored down Route 77 on one of their excursions from Boulder Lodge to Hayward in their Buick touring car, they noticed a sign for Moody's Camp.

Erle wondered out loud if it was the same Ted Moody who had worked as a mechanic on his car when they lived in the Dundee-

My father, David, and grandfather, Erle Oatman, show off their fine stringer of fish in front of Boulder Lodge, circa 1926.

Elgin area and decided to turn down Murphy Boulevard to check.

One can only speculate at the surprise and delight the two men shared upon greeting each other again in such an out-of-context setting. Ted and Myrtle proudly showed them around their camp, and the three Oatmans were smitten.

Clara especially liked the resort's elegant accoutrements over the more rustic furnishings of Boulder Lodge, and so without much further ado, Erle made plans to stay at Moody's the following summer. It was the beginning of a lifelong friendship between the families.

And what a discovery it was.

Erle, Clara, and David fell in love with it all: the splendor of the lake with its wild islands; the sunrises and moonrises across the bay; clear water and a sandy beach for swimming; challenging fishing; three delicious meals a day; and a bevy of interesting guests to befriend.

Clara and David were able to come north for as many as six weeks at a time, with Erle traveling back to Aurora to check on the dairy business as needed. It only took a few summers for the three to realize they wanted to stay forever.

Because of their close friendship, Ted and Myrtle offered to sell the Oatmans the first lot west of the resort. As one of the earliest private cabins built near Moody's, the property was graced with approximately 150 feet of shoreline that included a sandy swimming area and an acre of land. Erle and Clara knew it was perfect. They could have their own private cabin and still enjoy all that the resort had to offer: the fine dining, the use of the resort's help for chores, the fishing guides, and, most importantly, the friends. They were hooked.

And so, in the summer of 1929, Wake Robin was built. Clara designed it. Ted Moody and Hank Smith, a local Ojibwe, hand-crafted it inside and out.

Clara chose to name her cabin Wake Robin, the common name for the trillium, a white wildflower that blooms abundantly across the forest floor in springtime. With its delicate, three-pronged petals and serenely striped leaves, the Wake Robin wildflower perfectly encapsulated the spirit of their picturesque little cabin.

For despite their wealth and social status back in Aurora, the Oatmans sought simplicity in the woods. Like Thoreau (of whom Clara was an ardent admirer and reader), they appreciated the quiet humbleness of being close to nature and the strong sense of God's presence in the beauty that surrounded them. Choosing a spot high on a hill encircled with pine, oak, birch, and maple and with views of Big Spider's sparkling waters and islands, the Oatmans staked out their building site. Large granite boulders gathered from local fields and chiseled into sturdy squares served as a strong foundation, while nearby forests provided the cabin's long tamarack logs.

Clara and Erle decided a kitchen, two bedrooms, a living room with a fieldstone fireplace for warmth, and, best of all, a wind-cooled screened porch with a sleeping nook in the back were all they needed. Smith, renowned for his superb carpentry skills, hand hewed the logs and carved the chinking with the skill of an artist.

With a pump for water, kerosene lamps for light, a wood-burning stove for cooking, an icebox cooled by the previous winter's harvested ice, and an outhouse at the back of the property, the Oatmans felt Wake Robin was as charming and comfortable as any Northwoods retreat of the day could be. Delighted, Erle added a dapper straw bowler to his camp attire and Clara a straw boating bonnet to hers.

To celebrate the cabin's completion and the bond of their friendship, Ted presented Erle and Clara with an eight-point buck to hang over the rustic oak mantle as a housewarming gift. For all, it was a dream come true. Years of happiness beckoned.

Erle enjoyed fishing and relaxing amid the magnificence of the forest, which seemed to make the hassles of running a business quickly fade away; Clara reveled in the swimming and the birdsong that filled the air; David relished the freedom and possibilities for exploration that the woods and water offered a young

Left: My grandparents, Clara and Erle, circa 1933, on their dock alongside their square-stern canoe with its 3½-horsepower engine

Below: My grandfather's 1938 fishing license

boy. And eventually, when he received his very own boat as a teenager, it was the perfect place to grow into a man.

Savoring the unique blessings of their little cabin, they generously invited a multitude of close friends, including many of

David's, to share in the peace, adventure, and camaraderie of the Northwoods. On Mondays, they drove their Buick to Ashland in order for Erle to keep up his loyal attendance at the Rotary Club, taking in Lake Superior's spectacular views along the way. They dined at the lodge every night. They were blissfully happy.

And then, in the fall of 1938 at the peak of their bliss, tragedy struck.

Erle and Clara had just enjoyed their ninth summer at Wake Robin, where, for the first time, they had entertained David's college sweetheart and her family from Ohio for a wonderful month of togetherness. As was their tradition, Erle and Clara had stayed on to celebrate their September anniversary at the cabin surrounded by the brilliant changing colors of red and gold leaves that they so enjoyed.

Upon their return to Illinois, with Clara eagerly getting ready for the holidays and David off to graduate school at Ohio State University, Erle's heart suddenly gave out.

✂

I wonder if he knew it would be his last summer. Would he have done anything differently or kept it just the same? Perhaps that is the best way to leave the woods: to never have to knowingly say good-bye to the lake and forest forever.

I like to think he had one marvelous summer filled with all that he treasured. That the moon shone brightly, that the winds were soft, that the sunrises sparkled. Perhaps he caught a big musky, napped on the porch, laughed with friends, shared endless contented moments with his wife and son. I hope so.

But most of all, I wonder if he ever knew the legacy he would pass on. That David would marry that college sweetheart, that his five grandchildren would cherish the lake as he had, that his five great-grandchildren would do the same, and that, beyond all expectations, a fifth generation is now being joyfully introduced to the lake's still-wild allure.

Over the years, on one of the many endless all-day car trips Up North, when fatigue begins to set in and there are still several hours of driving left, I often ask aloud why Erle and Clara didn't stop earlier, especially since their ride took two days of travel over

My grandfather and father enjoy a moment on the lodge deck at Moody's Camp, circa 1929.

dusty, bumpy roads. Why travel 450 miles when 300 might have worked just as well?

Erle must have been asked the same question, for he was often known to remark, "You have to come this far north to get this kind of beauty."

And he was right. Like "The brightest star in the Milky Way," his love of the Northwoods shines on.

From a grandfather we never knew, that is quite a gift.

ON THIS FAIR BODY OF WATER

On this fair body of water

With its emerald islands fair

Where the sunshine is brighter

And the moon beams softer

Where the song of the bird is sweeter

And the tread of the deer lighter

Where the laugh of the child is clearer

And the hearts of the people sincerer

Will be wrought of the builder

From stone and log superior

A cabin called home (But it will be homier)

For in it will live a man worthier

A woman lovelier

And a boy heartier

Than any we know

Oh woods you are fortunate

To clasp in your arms such folks

They who appreciate and love your glory

Whose hearts and hands are tenderer

May you bless them in your prayer.

M.W.M.*

*M.W.M.—Meribel W. Merrill—was a great friend of the Oatmans from Aurora and a frequent visitor with her husband to Wake Robin. In the early 1930s, she wrote this poem on birch bark in black ink and illustrated it with sketches of Erle in a boat, Clara swimming, and young David fishing. It still hangs on the cabin wall.

Clara and the Cabin She Designed

1923–1957

"For the beauty of the earth / For the glory of the skies . . ."
—Old Gospel hymn

Clara.

I have always loved her name. There is a crisp elegance about it, and yet a softness, too. And that is exactly what she was like.

Her full name was Clarabelle Borden Oatman, which we five grandchildren found hilarious since there was a Clara Bell the Clown on one of our favorite television shows as kids growing up in the 1950s. We pondered the irony because no two personas could be less alike. Clara Bell the Clown was loud, silly, awkward. Clarabelle our grandmother was elegant, graceful, refined.

The comparison made us laugh out loud, and our grandmother laughed right along with us. To us, however, she was always "Grogey," the name with which my older sister Nancy christened her as a toddler.

It was only after Clara had been gone for many years, however, and I had matured into a young adult that I was able to hear and separate the lyrical loveliness of her given name from that of a cartoon character. *Clarabelle* beats in my heart with the sweetness of birdsong or the sway of a woodland flower.

She was both.

I adored my grandmother. To me, she was everything a grandmother should be: patient, fun, kind, encouraging, and fascinating in her own right.

For a woman born in 1876, she was highly educated, widely

read, and equally well versed in business, nature, and the arts. She was an expert in antiques as well as ornithology, a reader of Emerson, Thoreau, and Whittier, and an early devotee of Robert Frost. Her taste, no matter what the area, was exquisite.

It's no wonder she loved the Northwoods.

When my grandfather suggested they journey to the Hayward lakes area in 1923, she had no qualms about leaving an immaculate two-story stucco home filled with oriental rugs, oil paintings, elegant china, gleaming silver, fine linens, and a maid and climbing into an open-air touring car to travel for two days over gravel roads for the purpose of spending several weeks of "vacation" in a fishing camp with outhouses.

She was up for the adventure. Their young son, David, didn't need any convincing either. To the Northwoods they would go.

Although the Scheer brothers' Boulder Lodge resort provided a rough and wonderful introduction to the Northwoods for several summers, it was the discovery of Moody's Camp and all its charms that snagged my grandmother's undivided attention.

The white tablecloths, the wildflower bouquets, the food, the guests, the organized forest hikes through virgin pine, the picnics, and the "bathing" in the refreshing lake waters only fueled her lively intellect and fascination for life Up North.

Although she was wealthy, refined, and educated, Clara was no stuffed shirt. She possessed a wry sense of humor and delighted in the laughter and fun that made the Northwoods a perfect backdrop for all her varied interests.

The deep friendship she and Erle established with Ted and Myrtle Moody added to the ambience. It's no wonder she wanted to put down permanent roots by building her own cabin within a few short years. What could be finer than having a cabin of one's own while still enjoying all the attractive amenities that Moody's Camp had to offer?

As soon as Wake Robin was completed in 1929, Clara set about decorating it with all that she loved: Spode china, polished pressed glassware, stimulating books, antique rockers, opera glasses for bird watching, and, most beloved, her well-worn bird book for identification and sighting notes.

She cleverly blended birch leg tables, twig curtain rods, and

Right: My grand-parents on their newly constructed log steps at Wake Robin, 1929

wool hooked rugs with her finery, effectively avoiding a citified look. She used the same green paint as on the dock for the metal beds and outfitted the kitchen with the cream-colored, green-rimmed enamelware popular at the time. By combining the rustic beauty of the natural world with her sophisticated accents, she fashioned a warm and creative atmosphere for her cabin that enchanted all who entered.

And enter they did. Once settled, Clara, Erle, and David soon began to invite their many friends. Their 1931 guest book, inscribed with their three names in David's bold sixteen-year-old handwriting, includes more than forty signatures of family and friends in that summer alone, many of whom made the journey from the Chicago area.

With a wavy blond bob, twinkling blue eyes, and a vibrant personality to match, Clara was a generous and loving hostess—so much so that, as the guest book shows, many friends were frequent and repeat visitors.

Despite the rough and rugged nature of a cabin in the woods, which included kerosene lamplight, outhouses, fireplace heat, mosquitoes, spiders, and lake bathing, Clara did not abandon her elegance.

In summer, her signature style included floral silk dresses,

An early photo of Wake Robin's kitchen shows the original wood-burning stove, kerosene lanterns, teakettles, and dishpan.

sturdy white leather heels, pearls, and a swirl of diamond rings. When on the dock or in the rowboat, she donned her coquettish straw hat encircled with a navy blue ribbon; when temperatures dropped, especially in the fall, a stylish red leather jacket kept her warm.

But this wardrobe was almost contradictory to the activity she enjoyed most, for Clara loved to swim. Every morning, no matter how cold the weather or frigid the water, she slipped into her

swimsuit, donned her swim cap, and pulled on her white rubber "bathing shoes" for an early "dip" in the lake. And as on most other docks, a cake of soap was always on hand. Refreshed and invigorated, Clara was ready to start her day.

In such a manner and for nine splendid years, she and Erle lived their dream at Wake Robin. For them, it was the best of times.

✄

And then came the fall of 1938.

What a shock it must have been to have their time together at the cabin suddenly cut short just as they were heading into retirement. Clara and David were devastated. And yet, being a strong and independent woman, and no doubt making decisions in a way she felt would honor Erle, Clara bravely carried on and continued to make her summer pilgrimage to Wake Robin.

Clara and Myrtle Moody on the lodge porch, May 1931

For she was not afraid of solitude or being alone in the woods.

Bird watching, letter writing, reading, knitting, and, of course, swimming filled her days. Often for companionship she brought along her widowed older sister, Mina Borden Thompson, who

equally adored the Northwoods. The friendships of lake neighbors and annual guests at Moody's, whose company Clara enjoyed
while still dining nightly at the lodge, surely softened the sorrow
of Erle's death.

In the late 1940s and early 1950s when we five grandchildren
were born, Clara graciously gave my mother free rein at the cabin,
staying home when we were there in July and August. Loving the
early part of summer the best, Clara scheduled her visits from June
through the Fourth of July. Perhaps the commotion of our seven-
member family in her normally immaculate two-bedroom cabin
was a bit much to endure, especially after so much privacy.

Always independent, she continued to drive north each summer by herself until she was in her late seventies, when she finally
asked my father to drive her up and back. In 1956, my nine-year-
old sister Nancy was invited to go along as her companion. I was
green with envy.

Imagine my shock, however, when I was invited the following
year. In our family, to be picked to go solo with our grandmother
for several weeks at the cabin was a glorious surprise. Anticipating
the perfect mix of individual attention and independence, I knew,
even as a seven-year-old, it was a gift beyond compare.

My father drove us up in Clara's big black 1955 Buick, the two
of them in front and me contentedly in the back, luxuriating in

My grandmother knitting on the porch on a rainy day in the 1940s.

the lack of cramped chaos that usually accompanied our family drives Up North.

Once we arrived at the cabin, my father stayed just overnight to get us settled and then caught the next day's train out of Stanberry back to Illinois, where the many responsibilities of work and a large family awaited him. How he must have longed to stay on, if only for a few days, to enjoy the peace of the lake as well.

Before he left, my grandmother amazed me with three prettily wrapped presents. Sitting on the faded green canvas cushions of the porch swing, I felt like it was an early birthday as I unwrapped a baby doll to inspire my imagination; a game of Parcheesi for the two of us to play; and a red wooden whistle to call the birds, thereby introducing me to her feathered friends.

Perhaps Clara bequeathed these gifts to ensure my happiness, but she need not have worried. Being alone with her at the cabin was enough. As I blissfully swayed on the swing, my father kissed us good-bye, and Clara and I began our two weeks together in the woods.

><

Our days were simple.

While Clara savored the rigorous night air of the porch for sleeping, I enjoyed the cozy comfort of the double-bedroom off the kitchen—another luxury, since my two sisters and I shared a crowded bedroom back home.

As was her custom, Clara, even at age eighty-one, rose early to take her swim. Then, in common contentment, we shared a simple breakfast on the porch. Quietly listening to the wind-rustled leaves, we watched the sparkling waves dance across the lake in the brilliant morning sunshine. Surrounded by such blessed loveliness, it was easy to understand why her favorite hymn was "For the Beauty of the Earth," with its lyrics: "For the mystic harmony / Linking sense to sound and sight." I have never found a finer way to start the day.

After washing the dishes in the kitchen's green-rimmed enamel basin, we played a competitive match of Parcheesi or put the bird whistle to use out on the porch. Twisting the whistle's handle to attract the birds, I watched in wonder as robins, chickadees, and nuthatches suddenly appeared in nearby trees to sing their sweet song back to us. Afternoons were saved for dock time. As a novice swimmer, I watched Clara's elegant sidestroke and imitated her as best I could. She would step into deeper water, encouraging me into the safety of her arms and back out again. Like two playful otters, the octogenarian and seven-year-old, we floated side by side, buoyed by the waves and our comfortable camaraderie.

With so much activity to indulge in, somehow it wasn't long before the lodge bell rang out its first call to dinner at 5:00 p.m. sharp, and we knew it was time to dress for our evening meal. Recombing my lake hair up into a neat ponytail, I quickly stripped out of my swimsuit or shorts and changed into one of two carefully pressed cotton dresses while Clara donned her pearls. Together we climbed into her Buick for a stately drive down the dusty lane and up to the lodge. Warmly greeted by then resort owners Dick and

Lucile Seitz, we were escorted to our table for two overlooking the lake. As we dined on the evening's fancy fare, Clara shared pleasantries with the other guests, and I basked in the regal atmosphere as if I'd been crowned Queen of the Musky Festival.

Most treasured, however, was that, in addition to her daily individual attention, Clara gave me the blessing of independence. She trusted my choices and outings as long as I returned before 5:00 to get ready for dinner. I was free to walk the roads to the lodge by myself to investigate the day's activities, swim at Moody's beach as long as an adult was present, and chase frogs by the shoreline with my seven-year-old best buddy, Doug Seitz, the resort owners' son.

My happiness was complete.

And then one day my father appeared again, and I knew it was time to go home. As a young girl, I had no awareness of time gone by, and everything came to an abrupt halt. Suddenly we were packing up the Buick and swinging around the curve of the gravel road as the lodge bell tolled its sad farewell, its clanging resonance echoing through the woods, filling my heavy heart with the yearning to come back with her next year.

But for my grandmother it was not to be.

Perhaps times were too hard for my father to leave our family to drive her Up North. Perhaps the rustic setting was becoming too much. Perhaps she did not want to leave Mina, her frail older sister who lived with her, alone. All I know is that she did not go back again. A series of heart attacks took their toll, and she passed away in the spring of 1962.

Little did I know, looking back now more than a half century later, what our cherished time together at the cabin would mean to me. Through her quiet manner and simple acts of love, Clara instilled in me the wonder of wild birdsong, the thrill of independence, the gift of trust, the joy of simplicity, the imagination that is born of solitude, and the calm that comes with routine.

I can only hope that, in what turned out to be my grandmother's last summer at the lake, somehow my own seven-year-old self gave her as much happiness as she gave me. Mine has lasted a lifetime.

Sourdough Sam Sails On

1923–1975

"'What shall we do when hope is gone?. . .
"Sail on! sail on! sail on! and on!'"
—Joaquin Miller

He loved to laugh. And it was a good thing. For life didn't turn out exactly as he had hoped.

No doubt, David Borden Oatman's yearly sojourns to the Northwoods from the time he was a young boy until his death at age sixty-one gave him the strength, resilience, and peace he needed in later years.

One of the many reasons Erle and Clara Oatman decided to vacation in the Northwoods, or perhaps the main reason, is that they instinctively knew what a remarkable environment it would be for their young son, David. Such wild woodland surroundings would serve as a kind of counterculture to the more formal education and lifestyle back home in Illinois.

When they first vacationed in the Northwoods in the early 1920s, Erle and Clara surely felt that the whole of the great outdoors—woods, water, wildlife, rain, sunshine, moon, and stars—provided a perfect oasis for their eager son to grow, discover, and learn, and in the process make friends with others as well as with solitude.

He agreed.

It's no wonder that he became an Eagle Scout. His experiences in the Northwoods afforded him the opportunity to hone his outdoor survival skills and talents—so much so that he was chosen to serve in the Boy Scout Honor Guard at Roosevelt's 1933 inauguration in Washington, DC.

Although my father enjoyed the privileges and comfort that came with his family's wealth, he knew how to build a fire without a match, pitch a tent in the rain, swim with a strong steady stroke, serve as a lifeguard official, apply first aid, tie circles of complicated scout knots, and jury-rig anything that needed fixing. In addition, he possessed a creative flair as a whimsical cartoonist and artistic photographer.

Most of all, he loved fun and fun loved him. With his strong sense of humor, he appreciated the small ironies of life; observing the humorous, quirky oddities of humanity was his specialty.

To his elation, he discovered that the Northwoods was filled with the type of fascinating characters he so loved. The old-timers with their whiskers and hats who sat on Hayward's Main Street benches conversing about life were his favorites. He fondly referred to them as "Sourdough Sams" and, in a symbolic tip of the hat, he adopted that moniker in his own later years.

Blessed with Scotch-Irish good looks, my father's dark curly hair, smiling green eyes, and impish grin complemented a mischievous persona that often came into play. As a child growing up in Aurora, Illinois, he delighted in greasing the trolley cars' uphill tracks or planting a firecracker in a pile of dog poop just to see what would happen.

All his life, he was intrigued with the innards of car and boat engines, and no doubt as a young boy he found the two-day journey up to Big Spider Lake one big mechanical escapade. (Even years later, as a father of five with the seven of us stuffed in our station wagon and many roadside dilemmas to face, he never tired of the drive.)

As a teenager in the early 1930s, my father owned the fastest boat on Big Spider, courtesy of his parents. With his roguishly handsome looks, he zoomed around the lake like an Adonis on water. No dull dreamer, he used his ever-present inventive imagination to rev up the motor of his Century Cyclone with his own jazzy adjustments.

However, it was his engaging personality and sense of humor that made him a friend magnet. From his grade school years on up through Denison University, he established a circle of loyal friendships that would last a lifetime. Many of these friends, especially

three Sigma Chis who were as close as real brothers, would make many pilgrimages over the course of forty years to be together at Wake Robin.

My father as a young man, circa 1930s, ready to zoom off in his speedboat

It was when my father graduated from college that the world began to change for him. Up until that time, he had been blessed with seemingly charmed years. And then a series of events began to slowly dismantle the carefully built world that Erle and Clara had created for him.

Life must have seemed full of possibilities the summer of 1938: a college degree under his belt; a cabin visit from his college sweetheart and her family that suggested hints of marriage; plus the promise of graduate school at Ohio State University in the fall.

But with the heartbreaking death of his father in November, his plans were suddenly altered. Clara, widowed and with the dairy business to run, asked David to leave school and come home to help out. Being the devoted son, he did.

My grandparents
and father with
their dog, Peta, in
the woods by the
cabin, 1937

My grandparents and father with their dog, Peta, in the woods by the cabin, 1937

In 1944, David married that college sweetheart, Eleanor Alice Shumaker, aka "Woody," but shortly thereafter the army shipped him overseas to fight in the European theater.

How convenient that my father was serving somewhere in France. Although Clara was vice president of the company, a stock takeover by aggressive powers within the firm changed the direction and major ownership of the family business. My father returned to a completely reorganized firm that had slyly shifted him and Clara to minority stockholders.

Although my father eventually became vice president and a member of the board of directors of Oatman Brothers Inc., the new powers decided one cold day in the late 1950s to abruptly terminate that relationship. Without warning, my father was jobless with a wife and five young children to support. The promise of his father's company one day being his own, as Erle and Clara had planned, vanished in an instant.

Although he was able to find other work eventually, the shock, sense of failure, and personal loss all contributed to an escalating drinking problem. It took seven long years before he was able to finally free himself from alcoholism's clammy grip. During that time, Wake Robin continued to beckon as a sanctuary. Perhaps it was his lifesaver during those troubled years, offering a haven of

My father rows on
Big Spider Lake
after his return
from World War II,
circa 1946.

wild beauty, renewal, and calm. Surely my father's early years on
the lake and his scouting days were additional blessings that gave
him the survival skills he needed—in more ways than one.

Despite the many setbacks, my father and mother made every
attempt to keep the cabin and get all of us up there. Amazingly, we
did not miss a summer. With all the added financial difficulties, it
took a lot of extra hard work and sacrifice to keep Wake Robin going: taxes, bills, upkeep, and repairs, which were once easy issues,
now became a struggle.

Somehow, and with great effort, the cabin and our family
survived.

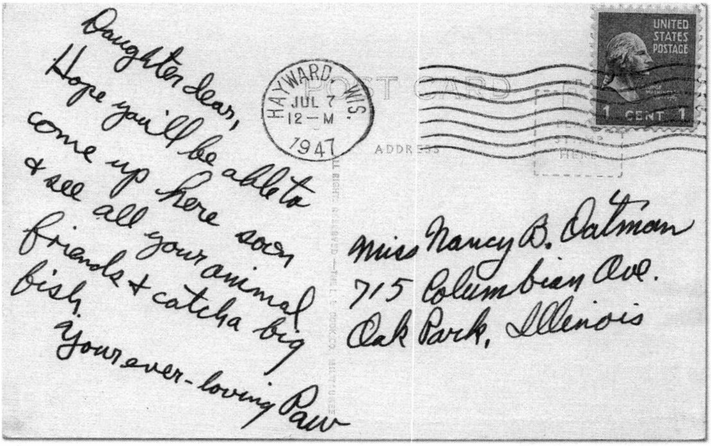

Daughter dear,
Hope you'll be able to
come up here soon
& see all your animal
friends + catcha big
fish.
Your ever-loving Paw

miss Nancy B. Oatman
715 Columbian Ave.
Oak Park, Illinois

HAYWARD, WIS.
JUL 7
12—M
1947

Regardless of our misfortunes, or perhaps because of them, we
continued to seek a silver lining. One fine summer, it arrived in
the form of a sailboat.

When lake neighbors announced they were selling their sleek
wooden Snipe, it was too good an opportunity to pass up. It took
$25 from each of my siblings' and my meager savings accounts,
plus our parents pinching back even more, to reach the $350 pur-
chase price. In honor of our group endeavor, we christened our
boat *Enterprise*.

It didn't matter that none of us knew how to sail. We would
learn.

My father was enthused by the challenge. Although the boat
possessed minuscule leaks, tricky rigging, and endless sand-
ing, painting and varnishing duties, my father was bound and
determined to become its skipper. Neither wind nor waves nor
a cobweb of unknown ropes could daunt his adventurous spirit.
He simply bought a book on the matter and studied up. On his
maiden voyage, he set sail by the seat of his white sailing pants,
book opened in one hand and the main sheet in the other. The
wind took hold, and away he went.

From then on, there was no turning back. And despite the

great effort and sacrifice of vacation time and energy that he and my mother undertook to get it ready to launch every summer, the *Enterprise* was just that: a family effort that, thankfully, generated good times together. Best of all, there was nothing like setting off on a soft sail to bring a sense of calm.

Over time we all learned to rig, tack, and sail, honing our skills to the many pleasures and challenges awaiting us on Big Spider's windswept water. Whether we were lazily singing and sunbathing with teenage friends on becalmed waters, scooting down the lake propelled by a brisk breeze, fleeing the raging winds of a storm chasing our backs, or surviving the drama of a rare capsize, we all thrilled to the sensation of getting in the boat and sailing away.

Perhaps that is also what my father loved most.

As any sailor can attest, there is a certain independence and joy that only the wind-and-water-powered momentum of sailing can create. Casting one's wits against rolling waves, whipping wind, or sultry calm to reach a destination is an exhilarating experience that by pure necessity often blocks out the worries and troubles of the day.

I think my father often found his peace out on the water. Whether he sailed alone or with friends and family, the pure act of rigging and running a sailboat allowed him to at last be master of his situation, to conquer the adversity of the elements, and to sail as one with the wind and nature. All the ugliness and sorrow of life gone awry was carried away on the breeze.

Perhaps, sailing along in those few blissful hours on the lake, he was able to jettison his personal demons and finally feel the freedom to believe in the person others knew him to be: funny, loving, kind, generous, and a darn good sailor.

Enterprise, circa 1960s

Gratefully, after his eventual recovery from alcoholism, his new job provided him with generous amounts of vacation time.

He used it all at the cabin—and getting *to* the cabin, including memorable trips in the late 1960s with chained-wrapped tires in midwinter when the temperatures hovered well below zero so we could ski at nearby Telemark. In a non-winterized cabin with no central heat or running water, it was essentially extreme camping. We loved it. Some of my family's fondest memories of Wake Robin are those wintry nights with frost on the logs, a coal fire in the stove, and the sound of my father getting up out of his own warm bed to throw another log in the fireplace to keep us comfortable.

How lovely it would have been if he had been able to enjoy a long stretch of recovery years and sail into a Northwoods retirement, joining the other Sourdoughs on Hayward's Main Street for a friendly chat. Sadly, it didn't turn out that way: eight years after recovering from alcoholism, he was struck with leukemia and died eight months later at age sixty-one.

Ironically, our sailboat *Enterprise* and my father ended their days on the lake around the same time. After the Seitzes sold the resort in 1967, we no longer had their helpful services to launch the sailboat's bulk. It became harder and harder to keep it seaworthy and, more often than not, its home was the log garage. Still, every time we rounded the bend to the cabin, its turtled bulk greeted us with a beloved reminder of those sublime sailing moments.

After our father died, our family made the executive decision, despite our deep sentimental attachment, to haul the *Enterprise* to the great sailboat heaven in the sky and took it to the dump, its worn and weakened frame long past repair. As with the end of all good symbols of a happiness, it was sad parting.

I like to think my father and his old sailboat friend have partnered together again somehow, and, like the eagles that often soar aloft on a wind current above Big Spider, so sails my father's spirit in a sunny breeze of freedom and peace.

Sail on, Sourdough Sam, sail on . . .

TO YOU I LEAVE

To you, I leave the woodland's lovely lyrics,
The shadowy paths where wild strawberries grow,
The robins' nests with safely sheltered fledglings;
Each stately tree that we have learned to know.

Across the lake, in the shimmer of the moonlight,
The loon's weird calling to his mate.
From the islands, and distant shore lines
The wild unfamiliar noises of the night.

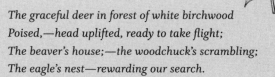

The graceful deer in forest of white birchwood
Poised,—head uplifted, ready to take flight;
The beaver's house;—the woodchuck's scrambling;
The eagle's nest—rewarding our search.

At morn's awakening—the bell like sound
of heavenly woodthrush
The plaintive pewee's call, the robin's rondalee
When day is done and night, softly falling
Brings peace and quiet—and all from care are free.

The glorious morning's sun red rising;
The stately blue heron's route—they always take—;
The solitary porcupine's quiet shamble
Along the paths that skirt the lake.

To you, I leave the lapping of the wavelets,
The soughing of the wind through distant pine;
The soothing silence,—the healing quiet,
All bring God's presence to a contented mind.

Mina Borden Thompson [Clara's sister], Wake Robin, 1930s

Wake Robin Welcomes Woody

1938–2008

> "If thou of fortune be bereft,
> And in thy store there be but left,
> Two loaves, sell one, and with the dole,
> Buy hyacinths to feed thy soul."
> —John Greenleaf Whittier

Woody and the woods were one.

The lake and forest spoke to her spirit, and she answered. Beginning in 1938 with her introduction to the Northwoods, courtesy of the Oatman family, she continually sought the beauty and opportunities it had to offer with a grand gusto. Adventure was her rallying cry:

"Who would like to swim to the island today?"

"Anyone want to canoe around the lake?"

"Let's hike back to Eagle's Nest!"

"Get up! Get up! The sunrise is glorious!"

Forget reading on the swing or taking a nap. Get going! For Woody, no day was long enough to capture all there was to see and do around the lake. A moment was not to be wasted.

And although we five children often sluggishly resisted her calls to activity, her contagious enthusiasm usually won us over. Once engaged, we knew we were in for a unique adventure.

><

Born in 1919, the redheaded Eleanor Alice Shumaker was soon nicknamed Woody after the famed Woody the Woodpecker character. And just like the echo of a woodpecker's happy *tap-tap-tapping* on a tree in the forest, Woody's arrival to the cabin signaled for decades that everyone's activity level was about to get kicked up a notch.

That was because for Woody, friends and family gathered together were the "hyacinths to feed thy soul." Whether it was a fish fry on the island, a picnic on the dock, a party on the porch, a hike through the forest, or a canoe trip down the Namekagon, the generous Woody was often the energetic organizer.

"It doesn't seem like summer until Woody arrives," our lake friends said repeatedly over the years.

And in truth, through the seven decades of her presence on Big Spider Lake, it didn't.

><

Like the first flaming rays of a sunrise, Woody's long, red hair no doubt captured David Borden Oatman's attention in the summer of 1937 when he was working as a lifeguard at Spring Valley Quarry in Granville, Ohio.

Woody relaxes on the dock in her Red Cross swimsuit during her first visit to Wake Robin in 1938.

My father always liked to say he attempted a fake rescue on my mother just so they could meet. It worked. With my mother entering Denison University as a freshman and my father a senior that

fall, they began their courtship
under the watchful eye of Woody's
father, Eri J. Shumaker, an English
professor at the school.

Love blossomed to the extent
that, by the end of the school
year, Dave had not only given
Woody his Sigma Chi fraternity
pin, but Erle and Clara Oatman
had even extended an invitation
to the entire Shumaker family to
visit them at their cabin on Big
Spider Lake.

It seems unusual nowadays to
have a whole family tag along just
to see your sweetheart, but in 1938
it was the proper thing to do. And
so Woody, chaperoned by her older
sister, mother, and father, set out
in early August for her first journey to the Northwoods. Because
the Shumakers were traveling so

far, Erle and Clara, always the gracious hosts, suggested they stay
a month.

Island picnics on Big Spider Lake were among the Northwoods pleasures my father introduced my mother to during her inaugural visit.

And so they did.

Accustomed to the high heat in the Ohio Valley, the Shumaker
clan packed only one light sweater each. Upon their arrival they
were shockingly welcomed to the crisp Northwoods air. Erle and
Clara's first task as hosts was to borrow an assortment of jackets
and wool sweaters from the Moodys and other lake friends for
their guests. Ironically, the cold Northwoods provided a warm and
humorous icebreaker for both families.

With jackets in hand, the Shumakers set up camp three doors
down at Clara's sister's cabin. Harry and Stella Borden Hemb had
recently built their own nearby cabin to join the family's rustic
adventure, as did many families of that era. Graciously, they allowed the Shumakers to use it in their absence.

With easy camaraderie, Erle and Eri were soon out fishing,

The Oatmans and Shumakers enjoy a lovely dinner at Moody's Camp during their month-long visit in 1938. Left to right: Woody Shumaker; Helen Shumaker, Woody's mother; Mina Borden Thompson, Clara's sister; Eri J. Shumaker, Woody's father; Clara Oatman; Marnie Shumaker, Woody's sister.

Helen and Clara were chatting on the dock, and David, Eleanor, and sister Marnie, were rowboating around the lake to view the water lilies and the loons. One by one, the Oatmans introduced their guests to all that they held most dear: dinners at the lodge, fires in the fireplace, visits on the porch, the sunrises, the star shine, the peace, the quiet. The Shumakers were smitten. Apparently, David and Woody were, too.

One of the highlights of their stay was the early celebration of Woody's nineteenth birthday on September 5. As red leaves began dotting the forest, signaling their vacation's end, the two families planned a party in her honor before they headed home. To accommodate all, the celebration was held next door at the cabin of Hedley Jobbins, a reclusive, generous entrepreneur and a friend of the Oatmans from Aurora.

It was a birthday Woody never forgot. And the only one she would spend with Erle.

Homemade birchbark candleholders lit the evening with lovely light, and wildflower bouquets filled the cabin with fragrant beauty. The families and friends shared fine food, laughter, lively tales, exuberant toasts to each other, and no doubt gratitude for the opportunity to be together. Woody's birthday party not only provided a festive way to conclude their stay but, for her, epitomized the beauty of nature and the fellowship of family and friends. (Seventy years later, gathering lake friends together was still the activity she treasured most.)

That first Northwoods sojourn must have worked, for after finishing college and working in Chicago as a corporate secretary, Woody married Dave on February 26, 1944. It was in 1946, on one of their first fall trips to the cabin after my father's return from World War II, that Woody casually announced that the hilly, rough roads were making her nauseous. One of David's lifelong friends, Bob Green, who was, along with his wife, traveling with them, kidded her that she was probably pregnant.

She was.

Nancy Borden Oatman was born the following May 25, with four siblings joining her within ten years: me, Margaret Prentice Oatman, born August 15, 1949; David Borden Oatman Jr., born October 31, 1951; Thomas Sanford Oatman, born June 29, 1954; and Mary Helen Oatman, born February 11, 1957.

And what better place to haul five active kids but to the Northwoods?

Wake Robin was waiting.

><

Vacationing Up North, however, means different things to different people. For some, it means quiet time on the dock, a book on the porch, a walk in a still forest, or a time to let the day unfold naturally.

But in our growing-up years in the 1950s and '60s, the Northwoods for Woody meant scheduling and planning. An organized canoe ride, swim, hike, sail, picnic, or party were frequently on her to-do list. She was not a sitter unless it was for a good visit on the dock. It's no wonder she often woke her five children at the crack of dawn to see the sunrise over the lake. What were we sleeping for?

In a moment of mischievous fun, our father wrote up a humorous schedule that perfectly parodied her daily desire for minute-by-minute activity. Tacked to the inside of a cabin cupboard for more than fifty years, it is a hilarious testament not only to my father's humor but also to my mother's energy.

In addition to her high energy level, Woody also believed the

AUNT WOODY'S SCHEDULE
for REST AND RELAXATION(?)

A.M.
4:45 RISE AND DO 50 PUSHUPS AT BEDSIDE

4:50 MORNING'S MORNING

4:55 SWIM TO ISLAND

5:05 100 PUSHUPS ON DOCK

5:15 JOG TO SAWMILL AND RETURN. TWO MILES

5:30 NATURE HIKE TO EAGLE'S NEST LAKE. COLLECT LEAF SAMPLES

6:00 CHOW (SPAM) ON DOCK

6:05 FLAG RAISING

6:10 ROW TO END OF LAKE

6:45 BIRD WATCHING CLASS NORTH LAKE

7:30 WASH CLOTHES

7:35 POLICE AREA

7:55 HORSEBACK RIDING

10:00 SWIM ACROSS LAKE

10:20 HUNT FROGS IN SWAMP

10:40 SWIM HOME

10:50 SAIL TO END OF LITTLE SPIDER

P.M.
12:00 COOKOUT ON ISLAND

12:10 EXPLORE AREA FOR FLORA AND FAUNA

1:00 WRITE THEME RE: FLORA AND FAUNA 750 WORDS OR MORE

1:45 FIVE MILE HIKE IN THE WOODS

2:30 FREE SWIM TO MUD LAKE AND RETURN

3:00 TAKE GARBAGE TO DUMP AND INTERVIEW BEARS FOR
       OPINIONS ON ROCK AND ROLL

3:45 WRITE THEME OF 1,000 WORDS ON BEARS

4:00 JOG TO MAIL BOX (SIX MILES)

4:15 PICK WILD FLOWERS

4:30 VISIT NEIGHBORS FOR HAPPY HOUR

5:55 SECURE INDIAN GUIDE FOR TRIP HOME FROM NEIGHBORS

6:00 CHOW

6:15 PRAYER MEETING

8:45 STAR GAZING FROM DOCK

9:30 FISH FOR MUSKY

10:30 CLEAN MUSKY

10:45 FREE TIME. WRITE HOME. WASH SOCKS

10:50 SAY PRAYERS

11:00 GO TO BED. ETC.?

We often started our day with an early morning swim—which also meant playing in the water. Here, my parents hold Tom and Mary, circa 1959.

more the merrier! Why not share all this Northwoods fun and beauty with others?

And so she generously invited entire families to come and stay with us at the cabin, often for several weeks at a time. It didn't matter that, frequently, all seven of us were already encamped. With only two small bedrooms, the twin beds on the porch, overflow sleeping in the rustic "guest room" connected to the back of the garage (where occasional bats hung out as well), and one tiny bathroom, she somehow made it work.

For several summers in the 1960s, my father's three best college friends—Ben Mellinger, Tom Allison, and Bob Deeter, all Sigma Chis and as close as real brothers—joined us with their families for a few weeks on the lake. Sometimes, one of the families stayed with us while the others stayed at Moody's cabins next door on the hill.

Our dock, however, was the gathering place. At different times of the day, it looked like an aircraft carrier landing strip as swimmers, sailors, fishermen, and canoeists zipped in and out while the sunbathers watched and visited. It's amazing the dock didn't collapse under the weight of so many. Despite all the activity and commotion, however, for my parents and these loyal, lifelong friends, it was a joyous time.

We children were also allowed to occasionally ask a friend to join us: our best friends from home, their parents, our neighbors, and my sister Nancy's and my boyfriends all made the trip.

With only a small refrigerator (a freezer eventually was added out in the garage storage room)—and despite the fact that gathering groceries meant a 40-mile round-trip to town with the five of us children in tow—Woody managed to entertain with creative flair and endless energy.

Her fish fries on the lake's several islands were legendary.

Woody would pack picnic baskets full of iron skillets, tablecloths, utensils, and her own special potato salad, which she'd gotten up at dawn to make. Hauling it all down to the lake, we kids and our father piled up our small fishing boat and canoe with enough supplies and firewood that by the time we all got in, the boats were barely floating above the waterline. It's a miracle we didn't capsize.

With a fleet of friends' boats and canoes anchored at an island's tip, Woody held court. Using us as assistants, she built the fire, fried up walleye fillets in a pound of butter, dished out her potato salad, and served homemade strawberry shortcake—sometimes even in pouring rain. When all guests had departed, satiated with laughter and food, she helped pack up the flame-blackened skillets and picnic paraphernalia, and—rather than return via a relaxing fishing boat ride—had enough energy to canoe back home with one of us kids as her partner (usually the one who did not make it into the fishing boat first).

When she wasn't entertaining, she happily supervised us down at the lake as we were never allowed to swim alone. It wasn't enough, however, for us to just fool around in the water and play.

"Who wants to swim to the island today?" she'd ask to no one in particular.

Swim to the island? Was she kidding? All we wanted to do was lie on the dock, get a suntan, splash in the lake, practice our cannonballs, or hunt for clams and frogs.

"I'll row," she offered.

And sooner or later one of us was usually coaxed into the effort. Once we got going, some of us swam to the island and back numerous times. As a teenager, however, Nancy won the prize by taking on the challenge of swimming, in rough waves, approximately half a mile across the lake. She did it.

Running Wake Robin like a camp, Woody put forth numerous goals for us to achieve: twenty-five laps in one session to the neighbor's dock and back; canoe around the entire shoreline; hike back through the virgin forest to Eagle's Nest Lake; row through the maze of water lilies to see their purple, yellow, and white blooms; get up and see the sunrise.

We were not always happy with these dictates and activities. Mumbling and grumbling often ensued. Why couldn't we just have hot dogs and potato chips on our picnics like regular kids instead of icky fish? Why couldn't we just sit on the dock and get a tan? Why couldn't we just be?

But once we were underway, we had to admit the canoe ride was fun, the swim to the island a new exploit to boast about, and the sunrise, of course, glorious.

The logistics of all this entertaining and activity were mind-boggling.

Grocery shopping was a major expedition. Not wanting to leave any of us at the lake for fear we might drown, Woody piled the five of us in the station wagon for the thirty-minute trip to town. Usually we were thrilled with an outing to Hayward, for it meant visits to all the intriguing shops: the dark, narrow aisles of Olson's Brothers for groceries; Pioneer Drugs for poison ivy lotion; and Wickland's Hardware for more of the fuses that, with so many of us at the cabin, we were always blowing. Like a bobbing batch of curious ducklings, we happily followed Woody's red head down Main Street.

Best of all, we sometimes would be allowed to roam around a bit by ourselves and check out the "Talking Indian" in front of the five-and-dime, get an ice cream treat at the drugstore soda fountain, or purchase a beaded deerskin coin wallet emblazoned with *Hayward* at the souvenir store with some saved quarters.

In the meantime, the laundry was piling up.

With seven people and no washer and dryer, Woody made the long drive—again, with her five children piled in the station

wagon—out to a farm in the country where a family operated a
laundry service in their garage. Several days later, we headed back
to pick up our many loads of sheets, towels, and clothes all neatly
wrapped in brown paper bundles and tied with string.

Up until around 1953, Woody gamely vacationed at the cabin
with three small children and only kerosene lanterns for lights.
She even ironed my sister's and my dresses for Moody's square
dances with an iron warmed on the wood-burning stove. But after
a bear scared her one night when she was alone with little Nancy,
baby David, and me, she decided it was time for the cabin to be

Woody reads
to me and Nancy
on the swing,
circa 1955.

wired for electricity. (Clara, however, felt Wake Robin's ambience
was never the same.)

Communication was another challenge, as our cabin, in keeping with its rustic character, had no phone. On the rare occasions
when someone needed to reach us, they called Moody's and our
phone messages were delivered via a chore boy. Consequently, if
Woody wanted to invite friends over for sugar cookies and lemonade on the dock, she either had to hike, boat, or send one of us kids
to deliver the message. Letter writing became a popular pastime

as the only means of communication with friends and family back home.

In addition to these basic workloads, Woody's annual specialty projects included attacking the lakeshore poison ivy with an arsenal of spray and scythes and devoting hours and hours to refurbishing the sailboat to keep it in seaworthy condition. We often found our mother lying on her back on the cool, mossy ground of the open garage scraping, painting, or varnishing the overturned sailboat.

Not exactly the definition of a vacation by most people's standards.

Woody cherished the time she had at the cabin no matter what the activity. Like the sunrise she so eagerly woke us up to see, she greeted each day with a glowing passion for woods, water, family, and friends.

Wake Robin: 2008
Her red hair is faded.

Soft white accents her temples like the gentle wisps of clouds on a blue-sky day. Legally blind, she can no longer clearly see her beloved stars or sunrises, and a walker is her steady companion.

It's been seventy years since Woody first arrived at Wake Robin as a young sweetheart. And except for the excuse of childbirth, she has rarely missed a summer—even after being widowed at age fifty-six more than thirty years ago.

For Woody, the love of a Northwoods adventure continues to beckon.

Her list of accomplishments over the years is a testament to her goal-setting determination: she canoed down the Brule at age seventy-eight; drove 800-plus miles from Ohio to the cabin by herself for twenty years until age eighty-one; swam in the crisp waters of Lake Superior on almost annual excursions until age eighty-two (it only counted if your head went under!); picnicked on the islands until age eighty-six; and at age eighty-eight willed herself to climb shakily down to the shore to get into a pontoon boat numerous times just for the chance to ride out on the lake and see the shoreline once again.

And to her friends and family, she is still the party queen. Lit by kerosene lamps on the porch, Woody's gracious fare and her cheerful hospitality are a welcoming delight to all who visit.

For the past decade, however, my sisters, Nancy and Mary, and I have taken on roles as Woody's designated drivers, cabin companions, and, most important, activity assistants. Woody's whirlwind social schedule, which includes visiting with friends or having them over—sometimes with as many as four gatherings in a day—keeps us on the move from the time we arrive until the time we leave weeks later. Reading on the swing or napping on the porch are still elusive pastimes.

As each year rolls by, though, Woody knows that her cherished time at Wake Robin is drawing to a close. Each year, toward the end of her vacation, she will softly announce, "This is probably my last summer. I don't know if I'll make it back." And so when it is finally time to leave at the end of another magnificent stay, our farewells to the lake and cabin and each other become harder and more poignant.

And so, as has become our custom on the morning of departure, my mother, sisters, and I stand in a circle on our sun-dappled cabin porch surrounded by the trees we know and love, and, with the whisper of soft waves lapping the shore, we hold each other's hands and one by one go around our little circle, offering a prayer of thanks:

"Thank you, God, especially for the beauty of your creation: the lakes, the woods, the stars, the moon, the sunrises, the sunsets, and the loon's lovely music that have meant so much to us."

"Lord, thank you for the gift of renewal to body, mind, and spirit, and for the clear sense of your ever-loving presence."

"Thank you for the opportunity and blessing to be all together again, for wonderful lake friends, and for all the fun, safe, and happy times we've shared."

"Thank you, God, for this little log cabin in the woods that we have cherished for so many, many years."

Then, shaking a little love around our clasped hands, we sing the old scout song:

"Oh, the Lord is good to me, / And so I thank the Lord, / For giving me the things I need, / The sun and the rain and the apple seed, / The Lord is good to me."

With tears, hugs, and kisses, we take one last look around the cabin and say good-bye. The packed car is waiting. It is time to go.

When the Seitzes sold Moody's Camp in 1967 and the big bell stopped ringing its fond farewells, we replaced it with our own tradition by clanging cowbells and shouting, "Happy trails! Happy trails!"

And so each year we send each other off with this wild racket. There is no finer way to leave the lake than to the happy shouts of beloved voices and the joyful ringing of bells echoing through the woods. As the car pulls around the bend with happy honks, Woody smiles and waves. She never looks back. As always, she turns and faces forward with optimism and hope. After all, another adventure just might be down the road.

She's sure of it.

In memory of "Woody"
Eleanor Alice Shumaker Oatman, 1919–2010

Heading Up North: A Journey in Five Acts

Circa 1959

"There's a long, long trail a-winding into the land of my dreams . . ."
—Stoddard King

Act I: Packing Up

SCENE 1

No one slept. Throughout the night we tossed and turned.

Outside the screens of our wide-open windows, cicadas sang the sweet song of summer, but as a lullaby, it did no good. The warm, humid air of an Illinois July night hung like a damp blanket across our bodies. Our suitcases stretched open at the foot of our beds, waiting for a sibling's bottom to sit on it and snap it shut.

Caches of Juicy Fruit gum and forbidden *Archie* and *Veronica* comic books were tucked away in discreet brown paper bags. Our beaded, deerskin coin purses, imprinted with *Hayward* and loaded with a tumble of small change, sat on our dresser tops ready to be stuffed into the back pockets of our shorts. We were ready. Dawn could not come fast enough.

We were going to the cabin.

My older sister Nancy, twelve, and my nine-year-old self lay in our twin beds, the sheets kicked off, whispering our excitement:

"I can't wait to jump off the dock into that cold water."

"And sleep on the porch."

"And go to the square dance."

"And picnic on the island."

"And see what friends are there."

On we jabbered.

Down the hall we could hear our two younger brothers, David, seven, and Tom, five, knocking against the wall and laughing. Our two-year-old baby sister, Mary, had been put to bed in her crib in our parents' room hours ago. The green illuminated dial of my Mickey Mouse watch told me it was past midnight, but the soft sounds of my father putting away pots and pans and my mother closing cupboard doors continued on in the kitchen, lending a muffled cadence to the night.

As the moisture-misted stars spun slowly over us in a haze of humidity, we finally fell into a fitful slumber, the hours ticking slowly by until the sound of our father's gentle voice suddenly pulled us from our topsy-turvy dreams of woods and water into the real adventure of the day.

Scene 2

"Uppy-uppy time!" rang out our father's cheerful voice. "Time to start packing the car!"

Nancy and I lay still for just a moment listening to the Aurora College church bells ring off the quarter hour, astonished that the sun was already peeking through our windows. Then, in the hope of an early start, we flew out of bed in a competition to beat the other to the bathroom.

One by one, my brothers and sisters and I stumbled into the kitchen, helping ourselves to the oatmeal bubbling on the stove courtesy of our father. Looking out the window from the long kitchen table, we could see that he had already turned our copper-colored, white-trimmed station wagon with its scooped-out tail-fins around and backed it down the driveway. The rear door hung open like the jaw of a hungry bear waiting for our wares. We were quick to oblige.

Like a bunch of busy beavers, we scurried back and forth from house to car, loading all our essentials. Our flurry of activity soon began to resemble an 8 mm movie in fast forward. In went pillows, suitcases, fishing rods, tennis rackets, sheets, towels, extra shoes, bags of groceries, books, games, canoe paddles, life jackets, hats, tools, and a loose assortment of eclectic items that seven family members felt were a "necessity" for a sojourn to the woods.

Stashed under the front seat were our emergency requisitions:

blue first-aid kit, red flares, green stainless-steel thermoses (one for hot coffee and one for cold water), white enamel boy and girl potty pots, and, most important, a brown paper bag filled with green grapes and orange chunks of cheddar cheese, our quintessential road snacks.

Before long, the back end of the station wagon looked like the human version of a beaver dam. My father's repeated requests for rearview-mirror visibility receded to a distant memory. Side mirrors would have to do.

Despite the fact that the back bumper was now hanging perilously close to the driveway, our treasured canoe—a Christmas gift from our grandmother Clara—still had to be hoisted on top of the car. Our mother and father each took an end, and with hefty huffs, heaved it skyward.

For a moment, the monster hung perilously in mid-air. And then, with a couple of good grunts, our parents steadied it and slowly slid it onto the two metal suction racks gripping the top of the station wagon.

There in all its hulking glory sat our long green canoe like a huge snapping turtle straddling a log. Its length spanned the entire vertical extent of the station wagon and then some. The stern blocked off our father's last hope for light from the back window and the bow dipped over the front hood like said turtle's beak in a feeding frenzy, splitting the front windshield's view in two.

Lord help us if we ever came upon anything in the middle of the road.

Checking and readjusting its balance, our father began to lash and whip the canoe to the car roof, zealously using dozens of ingenious knots he had learned when becoming an Eagle Scout. Neither rain, nor hail, nor hurricane-force winds would ever dislodge the canoe from that car. It would take the magic of Houdini—or our father—to untie those knots again, as we later always found out.

By now, it was mid-morning and we children were ready to hit the road. We jumped and twirled and scurried about, checking under beds and behind dressers for forgotten last-minute items to stash in any remaining crevices of the car. Our excitement and energy was at such a fever pitch that we could no longer stand it.

"Let's go!" we whined at intervals like a broken record player with a bad needle.

Our mother assured us she was almost ready; she just needed to tidy up and we'd be on the road. It would be her worst nightmare if we were all killed in a car crash and a stranger came into her home and found it a mess. Taking a quick look around, we instantly knew, of course, that our already delayed departure time was in deep trouble. Keeping a small, three-bedroom yellow ranch without a basement but filled with seven people free of clutter was no easy task.

And so the cleaning began. In an effort to speed the process, my siblings and I flew into conspirators' mode, sweeping books and toys under our beds, scooping clothes on the floor into the closets, and sliding the jumble of knickknacks on our dressers into the top drawers. Our mother felt she couldn't leave without vacuuming, which allowed our father more time to meticulously recheck the perilously overloaded tires and re-tie the knots.

By now, it was well past noon and we were starving. Our departure would have to be delayed further for a quick lunch. Out came peanut butter and jelly sandwiches and tomato soup. Nancy and I, uncharacteristically, readily helped with the dishes while

Our mother would not head Up North until the house was clean. Our great-aunt Mina's poem about Wake Robin is on the wall of our Illinois kitchen.

the boys chased each other around outside. Baby Mary sat in the grass and ate dirt.

At last, our dad began closing and locking all the windows of the house, checked the furnace for unknown reasons, and, finally, announced it was time to get in the car.

With happy whoops, the five of us scrambled to the sagging station wagon as our mother pulled the back door shut, locked it, and dropped the key into her black patent-leather purse. Sporting matching shoes and a linen dress, she liked to travel in style.

Climbing into the driver's seat, our dad took his first look into the rearview mirror, muttered an oath, and, with a shake of his head, gave up all hope of seeing out the back. Our mother tucked little Mary between them in the front as Nancy, David, Tom, and I made a mad jostle for the window seats in the back. Predictably, a fight broke out.

"I get the window!"

"No, you don't. You had it last time!"

"Knock it off," our father ordered. "You can take turns and switch after each stop."

Grumpily, we complied, not wanting to waste any more time.

"Fasten your seat belts!" Dad commanded.

"Do we have to?" I asked. "It's too crowded and hot."

"Fasten your seat belts and lock your doors," he repeated, leaving no room for argument.

Because cars of that era did not come with back seat belts, our father improvised, as usual, by creating two of his own and bolting them to the car floor. With four kids in the backseat, that meant two of us had to share. Stretching each belt across two bodies in order to snap them shut was no easy task, especially for sweaty, squirming brothers and sisters. Four sardines in a can couldn't have been any tighter.

I had no clue why we always had to lock our doors. There was no chance in hell we were going to fall out.

At long last, we were ready to go. Like a bunch of Cheshire cats, our forward-facing smiles all but exploded with excitement. Packed to the brim, loaded with seven people, and topped with a cavernous canoe, our station wagon careened out of the driveway like a 1959 version of the Trojan Horse and headed north. A huge grating noise and a blast of sparks from the laden back end rico-cheting off a driveway pothole gave us a rousing send off.

It was now past 2:00 in the afternoon, and more than 450 miles stretched before us. From the grip of my backseat snare, I studied my Mickey Mouse watch and figured, if all went well, it would take us about nine hours to get to the cabin. Surely, we'd arrive before midnight.

It never worked out that way.

Act II: So Happy Together
Scene 1

For a while, all was calm. We rode along in happy contentment, strapped in our shared seat belts, eager to watch the familiar land-marks glide in and out of view.

With the windows rolled down, the sweet smell of sun-warmed cornstalks swept through the car and cooled us with a tepid breeze as the green leaves of the cornfields waved a rustling farewell.

Crossing the railroad tracks of the neighboring town that sig-naled the start of our journey, we cruised by the familiar turquoise Rexall Drug sign and vintage redbrick storefronts and knew we were really and truly on our way. We were about to trade the sear-ing sun of the humid prairies for the cool shade of the forests.

Hallelujah!

It was time to crack open the Juicy Fruit gum and even share it with a sibling. Out came the secret caches of comic books and candy. We curiously, and with a bit of envy, eyed what the oth-ers had brought. Since gum chewing and reading were forbidden in the car due to our father's distinct dislike of the gum's sweet smell and our mother's fervid belief that reading in the car would make us go blind, we had to stealthily and silently unwrap our treasures.

Chewing with our mouths closed was one of our parents' con-stant manner mantras, so, for once, we tried to put that rule into practice in an attempt to hide our contraband. Due to our limited supply of gum, we were reluctant to share a whole stick, so with the magnanimity of a king or queen, we broke a piece in half and passed it around. (Our stinginess would later come back to haunt us when we ran out one by one.)

The *Veronica* and *Archie* comic books slid out from under a jacket or pillow. We looked over each other's shoulders, sneakily assessing the colorful pictures and snappy dialogue. Our father loved to drive, our mother to rest, and with little Mary sweetly snuggled between them, the four of us in the backseat silently read and chomped like contented cows chewing their cud and studying the soil. All was well with the world. We proceeded down the road like a happy caravan of traveling gypsies.

Then we got hot.

After an hour of blissful peacefulness, the afternoon summer sun began to take its toll and the shared seat belts were no longer a happy hug but a sweaty embrace. We began to stick to one another.

Off came the socks and the shoes, joining the mess of gum wrappers already crumpled on the car floor. Although the word had not yet been coined, our parents were early environmentalists, and we were forbidden to ever throw trash out the windows. Since we were sneaking the gum, we could not very well pass the wrappers to the trash bag in front, and so, guiltily, we tossed the paper remains beneath our seats.

In an outraged effort to shove a hot sibling away, we watched in horror as the gum, by now devoid of flavor, jettisoned out of our mouths and joined the tangle of shoes, socks, and wrappers below. As hard as we looked, we could never locate the gooey gunk until it maddeningly ended up stuck to one of us.

"Get off me!"

"Move over!"

"You smell!"

All of the above became our continual backseat whines.

"Knock it off!" our father commanded.

But the squirming and the sticking and the socking were there to stay. In addition, the dark green canoe perched heavily above us merely trapped more heat in our already packed and stacked station wagon. By now, all seven of us—our parents included—were beginning to squirm and sweat and sigh in the cramped confines of the car. It was all starting to sink in: we were stuck for at least another eight hours.

The initial euphoria of the trip blew out the window in a rush of hot, gum-smelling air as the two-lane highway loomed before us like the yellow-streaked back of a wiggling black snake.

Act III: Trouble Down the Road
SCENE 1
"Sing!" our mother commanded.

Our happy dispositions had evaporated like the heat waves on the blacktop, and we were now five crabby kids crammed in the belted seats of our steamy station wagon as it rolled down the highway.

"I'm happy when I'm hiking along the open trail!" Woody began in her strong soprano voice. "I'm happy when I'm hiking over trail and dale!"

"Come on now! Join in!" she insisted.

"I'm happy when I'm hiking . . ." we muttered with the enthusiasm of snared fish.

Gradually, the tune caught hold of our spirits and we finished the old scout song with a bit more life in our voices. After all, what else was there to do?

"Ten, twenty, thirty miles, fifty miles a day, hey!"

If it only took that long we'd be in heaven. Alas, we were barely into our northward journey, and hours of travel time loomed ahead. Our secret rations were depleted, Veronica and Archie's latest escapades were old news, and we had already pulled over twice for little Tom to "upchuck." Claiming carsickness, he was now happily ensconced in the coveted front seat next to the window.

We backseat riders were still stuck double in a single seat belt with baby Mary as a replacement. Her hard-soled, learning-to-walk shoes kept hitting us in the shins, and as the aroma of her suspected poopy diaper began reaching our noses, we were all the more cross and jealous of the new seating arrangements. Still stuck in the middle, I had yet to snag a window seat.

"Dip, dip, and swing them back, / Flashing like silver!" sang out our mother.

Now squished in the center seat next to my father with only a view of the canoe bow leading her down the highway, it was no wonder Woody chose this song.

"Swift as the wild goose flight, / Dip, dip, and swing. Dip, dip, and swing!"

"Come on! Let's sing it in a round!" she persisted.

Begrudgingly, Nancy and I mustered up our heroic Girl Scout attitudes and joined in the round.

"Dip, dip and swing 'em back, / Flashing like silver / Swift as the water flows / Dip, dip and swing / Dip, dip and swing."

As each round ended and the last voice faded out, we focused on the canoe above us, knowing that in not too long a time, it would be flipped back over into the cool, sparkling waters of Big Spider Lake, and we would be paddling the shore looking for real turtles on logs.

Our mood improved.

"Hundred bottles of beer on the wall / A hundred bottles of beer!" one of us mischievously sang out.

Promptly, without any encouragement, we all joined in with gusto. Here was a song we could really get into!

"Take one down, pass it around / Ninety-nine bottles of beer on the wall!" our voices sang, our loud laughter interrupting the refrain.

This was not one of Woody's approved scouting songs, and although we thought it was hysterical, we only managed to decrease to ninety-seven bottles of beer on the wall before we were abruptly cut off.

"That's enough!" she said, annoyed that her singing program had gone suddenly awry.

"Come on, Mom," we chorused. "It's just a silly song."

"No," she stated. "It's not allowed. Now, what else can we sing?"

Our answer was silence. In that tense standoff, someone's stomach growled, and we all realized we were starving again.

"I hungry!" said little Mary.

Our mother's traditional answer was to pull out the snack bag from under the seat and ration out chunks of cheddar cheese and green grapes. We snatched them up in an attempt to quench our endless hunger. Consequently, there were now smashed grapes and chunks of dried cheese amid the shoe-and-sock-strewn car floor with chewed gum and candy wrappers scattered throughout. It was beginning to look like a dump down there.

Our complaining started up again.

"I'm thirsty!"

"Me, too!"

"I've got to go to the bathroom!"

"When are we going to stop?"

"As soon as we find the next filling station," our father patiently answered. "Keep your shirts on."

Restlessly, we scanned the horizon for the answer to our prayers; the red, white, and blue crown of the Standard Oil gas station. But instead, only fields of black-and-white Holsteins, faded red barns with fieldstone foundations, and colorful waves of roadside wildflowers stretched out for miles around us.

Suddenly, the whole car began to shake and a persistent *thump-thump-thump* joined the highway sounds of rushing wind and whistling road like a symphony drum beat gone awry.

"Damn!" cursed my father under his breath.

"What's wrong?" we asked in quick dismay, wondering if the canoe was about to flip from its suction cups.

"We've got a flat tire," he answered, resignation in his voice.

Not again, I thought to myself.

For once, all voices were hushed and a suspenseful silence filled the car as we anxiously watched our father guide our loaded station wagon expertly off the road onto the gravel shoulder. Coming to a rude halt, the car gave a sighing shutter as the engine shut off. An unaccustomed stillness followed.

Hot dust drifted up around us from the gravel and dirt. New noises of chirping crickets and buzzing bees rang out from the eerie quiet that greeted us through the open windows. Collectively, we sighed.

We were stuck.

"All right," our dad ordered. "Everyone out and stay away from the road."

Happy to at last be released from our seat belts, we scrambled to find our shoes and socks in the mix on the floor.

"Darn it!" I hollered glaring at the nearest sibling. "I've got someone's gum stuck all over my shoe."

"Find a leaf and wipe it off," Woody answered. "Nancy, you keep an eye on Mary while I help your father."

"I think I'm going to upchuck!" Tom announced, eyes wide and face pale.

"Marnie, watch your brother," Dad ordered.

For once, I hoped my kid brother was faking.

Scrambling out of the car, we gathered near the back end to take a look at the offending tire. There it sat in wrinkled reverie, the black rubber deflated to the rim, the head of a large nail protruding from its worn treads.

"Damn!" our father muttered again.

Our gazes uniformly shifted slowly upward to the canoe anchoring the back end shut where the spare, of course, was located under all our stuff. Securely knotted to the car like a green bug ensnared in the intricate clutches of a spider's web, that canoe was not going anywhere fast.

We were going to be here a while.

Act IV: Calling the Cows
Scene 1

Buzzing mosquitoes attacked immediately. Standing in the hot, late afternoon sun on an empty road miles from nowhere, we stood in shocked silence swatting the stinging pests away.

The spare tire, of course, was not only beneath the gargantuan mountain of luggage in the backend, but the canoe had to be released from its carrier before the back door could swing open to retrieve it.

Gazing at our father's endless array of complicated canoe knots, we realized they had succumbed to Isaacs's law of physics: for every action there is an opposite and equal reaction. The buffeting winds that the car had careened into for several hundred miles made all those knots tighter than a sailor's hitch in a hurricane.

Instinctively, we knew it would take ages to get them all undone. And it did.

Although it was still sunny out and there was not a car in sight, our father, the ever-safety-minded Eagle Scout, retrieved his stash of flares from under the front seat and placed them in the hot tar cracks of the pavement at the front and back of the car.

Fascinated, we kids paid close attention, for this was our favorite part (we'd been down this road before, so to speak). With great fanfare, our father pulled his stainless-steel cigarette lighter out of his pocket, flicked the lid back with a flourish, and ignited the flare wick.

"Stand back!" he ordered, as though an explosion were imminent.

As the small flame took hold, he leaped back like a man who has just thrown a grenade. Sizzling and hissing like a cornered snake, the wick suddenly exploded into a firecracker burst of red sparks.

Happily, for a fleeting moment, changing a flat tire resembled the Fourth of July. But just as quickly, we were back to the matter at hand: untying tight knots and emptying our overpacked car.

Eventually, the canoe was freed from its bindings and lifted off. Like a movie in reverse from the morning's packing, we one by one piled all our traveling paraphernalia into the canoe's hull now beached on the roadside gravel.

Before long, the urgency of why we wanted to stop in the first place returned in full force. Where was that gas station restroom when we needed it? The dreaded potty pots were our only recourse.

Out from under the car seat came the roll of toilet paper that Woody had discreetly placed there. Using the open car door as a screen, the first user hollered out a warning: "Don't anybody look or I'll sock you one!"

Despite the fact that for miles the only audience was cows and birds, in a family of seven, we sought out any privacy we could find on a deserted highway surrounded by pastures.

Before long, our dad was able to dig out the spare tire and the jack from its hold under the station wagon floor and set the contraption to work. Slowly the back end of the car rose like an ornery phoenix from the ashes.

Tired of throwing rocks and watching the Holsteins in the nearby field, we now gathered round to observe our father loosen the bolts of the offending tire. They too were tightened as taut as a screw in a submarine. There was no chance in hell that tire was going to roll off and crack a cow unawares.

"Here, hold this bolt," Dad ordered as he handed one to each of us. "And whatever you do, don't lose it!"

We clutched our bolts in our sweaty hands, mesmerized by the slowly turning tire. At last, with a few hard yanks, off it popped from its grisly grip.

Suddenly out of the quiet country air came the far off rumble of an exhaust pipe. Waiting in wonder, we watched as an old pickup truck came trudging down the road. Embarrassed by our situation and a little bit fearful, we were nevertheless curious to see who was coming our way.

Woody instinctively gathered baby Mary up in her arms. The rest of us kids stood at high alert, a little nearer to each other, ears perked, all eyes focused left as the cloud of dust drew near. We were ready to bolt if needed. Gradually, the rusted, beat-up truck came to a grinding stop beside us.

"Need any help?" asked a gray-whiskered farmer through his rolled down window, a worn and faded fedora tipped back from his sunburned face.

"Thanks, but I think we just about got it," Dad replied.

"I seen your flares from across the field," the farmer added. "Looks like you been here a while."

"Yes, but we're almost through," our mother warily offered.

"Well, I see ya got some fine helpers," he added, giving us a wink.

"Yes, we do," our mother replied.

"How far ya'll going?" he asked.

"Up near Hayward," our father answered as he pulled a pack of Lucky Strikes out of his top pocket along with his ever-handy lighter. Leaning against the hood of the truck, he lit his cigarette and took a long pull, happy for a chat with an interesting character.

We rolled our eyes, knowing our delay just got a little bit longer.

"You got a ways to go then," the farmer said as he assessed the late afternoon light. "And it don't look like you're gonna make it before dark either."

"No, we got a bit of a late start," Woody confessed.

"Well there's gas station about ten miles up ahead where you can get your tire patched," he added. "But if you have any more trouble, our house is back down the road about a mile."

"Much obliged," Dad answered.

"It's beautiful country up yonder," the farmer added. "Used to fish theres myself back when I was a kid. You kids lookin' to go swimming?"

Our heads nodded in silent unison like puppets on a string. Now covered in dust and sweat, we realized our hopes of jumping off our dock into a cold lake on this hot summer day were about as real as a mirage in the desert.

"Well, I won't keep you any longer," the farmer said, a smile cracking his weathered face. Slowly he scanned the scene one more time as though he couldn't believe his eyes: five kids, a flat tire, and a canoe overflowing with vacation junk. Smiling, he nodded his head in farewell.

"Good luck!" he called.

Tipping down his fedora, he pulled the truck forward a few yards, backed it carefully around the flares, and headed down the road in the opposite direction.

"Well, he was a nice Old Sourdough," said Dad, now rested and relaxed from his visit.

We nodded in agreement, just thankful we hadn't all been murdered.

"Now hand me your bolts, and we'll get out of here," Dad ordered.

In all the excitement, one of us turned up empty handed. Dad only shook his head, took a deep breath, and gave the remaining bolts one last tight twist. Our mother passed out the last of the green grapes and cheddar cheese, which we gratefully washed down with a tepid swig from the near-empty water thermos.

As the sun began to drop toward the horizon, we stuffed all our belongings back into the rear of the station wagon, cramming them in with no thought of order. With an exhausted heave, our mother and father lifted the emptied canoe back up to its berth. Dad resecured the knots like he was in a scouting speed competition, put out and restashed the almost burned-down flares, and packed the jack under the front seat just in case. At last, we were ready to go.

There was just one last thing to do.

"Oh, Dad, please call the cows," we pleaded, not wanting this chance to slip by.

"Alright," he said, needing little encouragement.

Cupping his hands to his mouth, he issued forth a long, deep bellow that gradually crescendoed in volume and pitch.

"MoooooooOOOOO!"

One by one the cows raised their heads and, as if hypnotized, began to saunter forth in our direction.

Pleased at his first cow-calling success, our father let loose with another mournful "MoooooooOOOOO!" Lo and behold, the cows picked up their pace and started to run! Our father mooed some more and soon we had a bevy of bovines all eyeing us up close and personal over the top of the fence. We laughed ourselves silly.

Practicing our own moo calls, we kids watched as the last of the herd wandered over to see what was up. Then with happy hops, we headed back to the car to resume our Northwoods voyage.

"Seat belts!" our father ordered as we snapped ourselves once again into that taut torture device. "And lock your doors!"

We did as we were told—there was no point in arguing this far into our journey.

Our mother now slid behind the wheel, giving our dad a chance to rest. Bellowing a parting "MoooooooOOOOO!" from his window seat, Dad locked himself into his seat belt just as our mother inadvertently stepped on the gas and peeled us out of there in a flurry of rocks and dust.

"Geeze, Woody!" our father muttered. "Slow down!"

The car swayed wildly as our mother adjusted to the canoe's top-heavy weight and then steadied as she headed determinedly down the highway. Sticking our heads out the car windows, we laughed and mooed farewell to the puzzled dark-eyed cows receding into the distance.

SCENE 2

On a hilltop across the field, a farmhouse light blinked on. Thinking he heard the odd sound of mooing laughter, the farmer washing up at his kitchen sink looked out across his cow-filled meadows just in time to see a canoe-crowned station wagon careen over the top of a hill, its back bumper spitting off a shower of sparks as it scraped the crest of the blacktop before dipping down out of sight.

"I'll be damned," he mumbled, checking his watch. "They sure ain't gonna get there by midnight.

"Millie, is supper ready yet?" he asked, laughing. "You won't believe what I saw on the road today."

Act V: Are We There Yet?
Scene 1

Dusk drifted over the fields like a cozy quilt as we settled in for the duration of our trip.

Out the car windows, the light faded from blue to lavender to a burnished gray. The last red rays of the setting sun coated a crest of cumulus clouds riding the horizon like waves pulled by moon tide.

Our low-slung, bug-encrusted car slid through one little town after another with signs pointing to the familiar names: Augusta, Cadott, Cornell, Ladysmith. Passing by tidy clapboard homes with cement-deer yard art, we watched the golden glow of kitchen lights click on one by one like lightning bugs in a summer field.

Slowing to the speed limit of the deserted main streets, we could feel the heat still emanating from the low brick buildings as though they were sun-warmed canyon walls. Above us, the soft amber of streetlights provided a brief, hazy snapshot of darkened storefront windows. As we headed back out into the cooling country-side, neon signs in bright hues of red, yellow, orange, green, and blue sporadically popped out of the darkening forest like woodland ghosts with their simple offers of "Vacancy" for the weary, "Food" for the hungry, and "Beer" for the thirsty.

Soon, favorite landmarks became more recognizable, suggesting we were *definitely* making headway. There was the corner Standard Oil gas station with its red, thirst-quenching Coca-Cola cooler standing sentry by the garage door; here was the largest cottonwood log in the county, its many circles of rings begging to be climbed on; there was our mother's cherished pie café that simply said "Eat"; and best of all, here came the old schoolhouse with its tempting set of swings where our father, when needing a rest, often stopped to let us play.

All were places we frequented on our trips Up North, visiting as needs and time dictated. But at this late stage in the day, we didn't mind passing them up.

On we cruised down the black ribbon of our two-lane highway, the dark filling up the fields and forest so that only the yellow beam of our headlights marked the way. Silhouettes of barns and trees and fence posts were all that stood out in the dimming twilight.

We were tired now.

The nail-spiked tire had been duly patched at our last gas station stop, and we had sunk into a kind of resigned waiting. The car became quieter and our heads began to nod.

At last, one of us spotted the orange lights of the tiny A&W Root Beer stand up ahead. We poked and ruffled each other awake, our mouths salivating at the thought of cheeseburgers, fries, and frosty root beers. As soon as our dad pulled into a stall under the bare, bug-encircled light bulbs, we clicked out of our seat belts. Eagerly, we watched the waitress reluctantly dislodge herself from the cook's window and expertly approach us on a slick pair of white roller skates.

Ducking her white cap down under the driver's side window, she uttered a surprised "Hello" at the sight of our disheveled station wagon crammed with seven people.

"What can I get you?" she asked, pencil and pad poised at the ready.

In an instant, all hell broke loose.

"I want onions rings!"

"Don't give me any pickles!"

"Get me a chocolate shake!"

"No mustard!"

Knowing we'd be there forever with so many individual requests, our father expedited the process by ordering the same for all of us. Seven burgers with everything, seven fries, seven root beers.

"I hate all that stuff on my burger!" I snarled under my breath.

A popular stop for my family on our long journey from Illinois to north-western Wisconsin: the A&W Root Beer stand in Augusta. My mother always wore her traveling clothes, includ-ing pearls and spectator pumps, for the arduous drive to the rustic Northwoods. In stark contrast, we children grabbed whatever clothes were at hand, such was our excitement to get on the road. Circa 1958, left to right: David, Tom, Nancy, our mother holding Mary, and me.

"You can scrape off what you don't like," he said ignoring our grumbling from the backseat.

Too hungry to argue, we sat back in stomach-growling antici-pation. Patiently breathing in the greasy scent of fried onions, we listened to the chirping crickets sing out from the dark as though they were the designated dinner music for our feast.

After what seemed like an eternity, our waitress rolled up with an overflowing tray, snapped it to Dad's side window, then made a return trip for another load, anchoring it to Mother's side. Chaos erupted as our parents passed out the mouthwatering fare. Except for the waitress laughing at the cook's window, silence ensued.

Pickles, onions, mustard, and ketchup never tasted so good.

SCENE 2

It was cooler now.

The night breeze drifted in through the car, carrying hints

of pine and leafy woods. We rolled our windows up a bit higher and snuggled next to each other, for once glad for a sibling's cozy warmth.

Quiet settled over the car as we stuffed pillows behind our heads and spread shared jackets over our knees. Knowing the nearness of the cabin, we became peaceful. Our father was back behind the wheel, smoothly hugging the curves and hills of the changing terrain. Now that the view was dark, I had finally secured a coveted window seat. Tipping my head back, however, I could look up through the shadowy overhang of trees and watch the sparkling stars slide across the heavens.

As we came upon open pastures, the stars burst out in glistening glory like God's own flares across a celestial highway. The Big Dipper hung above us, anchoring the constellations of the night sky. And like a rosy ripe apricot, the full moon climbed slowly out of the misted forest.

We were almost there.

By now it was well past midnight, the highway empty except for the occasional gleam of an animal's eyes reflecting from the side of the road. Only the ghostly white stripe of the road's center served as our guide. Houses and barns stood darkly in their clearings, illuminated by a lone yard light.

The greenish glow of the dashboard cast an eerie iridescence across the sleeping faces of our mother and baby Mary, again in the front seat. The four of us in the back sat in crumpled repose, still gripped by our shared seat belts.

Gazing out the window into the silver-shadowed night, I felt suddenly familiar with the road, as if I was waking up in a well-known room. Was it the curve of the blacktop? The arch of the trees? The recognized shape of a glacial boulder? Somehow, in the pit of my stomach I sensed a closeness to the cabin, and my heart flooded with joy.

"Daddy, are we almost there?" I whispered.

"Yes, sweetie, we are," he answered softly. "It won't be long now."

Alertly, I watched as we rounded a series of curves and hills, each becoming more recognizable, like a well-loved face not seen for a while. Then, almost imperceptibly, the car slowed as we coasted down a hill to a one-lane silver-railed bridge.

"We're at the bridge!" I whispered to my backseat siblings. "Wake up! We're at the bridge!"

The inside of the car sprang to life like a jack-in-the-box. As was our tradition, our father stopped the car smack in the middle of the bridge, and we cranked our windows down as fast as possible.

Breathing in great gulps of the crisp, clear Northwoods air, we craned our necks over each other to get a good look. To the left, the wide vista of North Lake opened up before us with sparkling Cassiopeia reigning regally above in her throne. To the right flowed the meandering curves of the water lily–studded thoroughfare, its border of heart-shaped lily pads reflecting the moonlight. We stared out in wonder at this wild beauty, not knowing where to rest our gaze, such was its loveliness.

Anticipation hung in the air as our father inched the car forward onto the crunch of gravel road and under the tall, welcoming, log "Ted Moody's Camp" sign.

"We're almost there! We're almost there!" we whispered, awed by the magic of the moment.

Ignoring our safety rules, we at last clicked off our seat belts and piled on top of each other for a glimpse of cherished landmarks. As we came into the clearing, we saw the wide stretch of tennis courts with their dipping nets. Behind them sat the rambling log lodge with its large cast-iron bell softly silhouetted by the light over the kitchen door. The long-roped tree swing still hung from its high branch, and several picnic tables circled the fieldstone grill as if recently used.

To the right loomed the dark shadows of Eddie-the-fishing-guide's shack and the log carport garage with a room above. Our canoe-capped station wagon slid slowly past it all like a midnight monster on the prowl.

Our father eased the station wagon down a steep, deeply rutted gravel hill, the car dipping and rocking with every bump and ridge. At the bottom, the road forked, and the car swung right onto a one-lane, grass-centered dirt road; its twin, the "high road," ran parallel to the left. As we crawled up the long, low hill, our anticipation propelled us to the edges of our seats. Swinging around

Our station wagon, late 1950s, was often topped with a canoe for our trip Up North.

a curve, the car slid under the gracefully arching branches of a white birch.

At last, there before us waited all that we had longed for.

The car lights swept past our old log garage with our sailboat, the *Enterprise,* upside down on the mossy floor. Up into our woods the headlights beamed, then down a little hill where our cherished log cabin sat in all its simple glory. There, it rested peacefully in the moonlight, as if it had been patiently waiting all along for this burst of life that was suddenly upon it.

Our dusty, insect-adorned station wagon halted wearily by the cabin's back door. Our father turned off the car, and the echoing clinks and clangs of the overheated engine faded into the welcoming silence of the still night.

In that instant, our contained excitement burst forth like the flares we had lit earlier in the afternoon.

"We're here! We're here!" we shouted.

"Shhhhhh!" our mother scolded. "Don't wake the neighbors!"

The car doors burst open and we tumbled out. Even in the moonlight, we could see the beam of each other's smiles. Fragrant pine air greeted us with its cool, welcoming balm. We scrambled to find that one lost shoe, then gave up in our hurry to get into the cabin.

"Don't slam the car doors!" our father admonished.

Too late. In our rush of enthusiasm, we carelessly banged them shut.

Down the fern-lined stone-and-log steps we laughed, racing to be the first to open the leaf-strewn back door. Piling into the narrow hallway, we stood in a row in the darkness as our father searched for his key. Standing in silent unity, we breathed deeply of the musty log scent, our hearts filling with happiness.

Finally, we were here.

And then the door swung open, and we rushed into the cabin's dim darkness.

"We get the boys' room!" my brothers yelled.

"We get the porch!" my sister and I answered.

Spanning out, we took in all our beloved details: the green breadbox with its colorful little painted maiden dancing amid her flowers; the kitchen table tacked with its red-checkered oil cloth; the white-and-black enamel stove with its antique copper kettle and tin coffeepot waiting on the back burners for a hot brew. We peeked into the bedroom to the left with the green metal double bed and matching dresser and mirror and then skipped over to the bedroom on the right with its twin beds and twigged curtain rods draped with our grandmother's original wooden-ringed cotton curtains.

Satiating our curiosity that all was as we had left it, on we flowed like a troop of ants into the living room, where the eight-point buck seemed to wink a welcoming smile from his mount high over the mantle. One of us slipped the leather tong latch from the heavy wooden door's iron holder, and we streamed into the porch's lovely dampness.

Below us glistened the moonlit waters of Big Spider Lake. From our porch perch on the hill, we heard the gentle break of waves on the shoreline calling to us with its midnight splendor.

"Can we go down to the lake?" we asked our mother.

"If you go quietly," she said.

"Take this flashlight and watch each other," our father added. "I'll plug in the fuses and the lights will be on in a few minutes."

Leaving baby Mary back with our mother, the four of us joyfully stumbled down the log steps, the leader occasionally remembering to shine the flashlight forward and backward so that we all might see and not fall. Spilling out onto our dock, we surveyed the beauty of the night. By now, the moon had climbed high into the sky, outlining the magnificence of the lovely long island stretched out in front of us; to the north rested the clear silhouette of the tiny island we'd named Sunrise Island, and far across the shore blinked the yard light from Hans Roost Resort.

Most of the cabins were sleeping quietly in the dark, so we could only wonder which lake friends might be up. As we peered intently into the moonlit water, we were reassured to see the brawny boulders that served as our stepping-stones for swimming still in their rightful place.

We always relished the chance to sail on Big Spider Lake on the *Enterprise* after our 450-mile drive to Wake Robin. Here we are, left to right, in the early 1960s: Nancy, Mary, me, David, and Tom.

Standing side by side in a shared sense of camaraderie, we gazed out at the dancing path of moonlight that crossed the lake to exactly where we stood on the dock, as though it were a straight link from heaven above. Tilting our heads back, we drank in the majesty of the twinkling stars sparkling against the backdrop of black velvet sky, a million times brighter than we ever saw them back home. A soft lake breeze brushed our cheeks like angel wings.

Suddenly, the lights winked on in the cabin, and our father switched on the outside light to guide our way back up.

"Come on up now," he gently called. "It's past 2 o'clock. We'll unpack the car in the morning."

Racing up the steps to our awaiting beds, we recognized even as young children, how blessed we were to be back again. Abounding gratefulness was our prayer as we climbed into chilly sheets under wool World War II blankets. Soon the quiet calm of the forest enfolded us, and the steamy cornfields that initiated our long odyssey vaporized like a dream into the cool night air.

A loon's lullaby filled the night. As we drifted off to sleep, we knew a peace like none other.

Moody's Camp Changes Hands

The Dick and Lucile Seitz Era, 1955–1967

"To affect the quality of the day, that is the highest of arts."
—Henry David Thoreau

It was their dance.

Like two shimmering dragonflies, they swirled with ease around the makeshift dining room dance floor to the lilt of a lively waltz.

The scent of the fresh pine boughs that graced the ceiling's log beams drifted through the warm, moist air as square-dancing guests from the resort and neighbors from around the lake settled into clustered hickory-backed chairs hoping to catch their breath and be cooled by lake air drifting through the open windows.

Gradually, the chatter of these onlookers subsided as they became mesmerized by the lone couple on the floor. Within a few moments, the only sound was the strumming of the band—accordion, guitar, and drums—and the soft slide of the dancers' shoes.

Tall and lean, he held her firmly in his arms, his gentle blue eyes locked into hers as they glided effortlessly around the room. Her pleated petticoat skirts swirled and swished with each graceful step. Occasionally they both glanced away to smile at their guests, but mostly they looked at each other.

Even this ten-year-old girl recognized something special was happening, for as the two dancers floated across the maple wood floor to the accordion melody, they emanated a sense of love and delight that would be hard to miss in this Northwoods setting.

For them, such intimate moments must have been all too brief. For tomorrow they would be up with the sunrise's first golden light, facing the daunting demands of running a resort.

But tonight they danced.

><

It would not be far-fetched to claim that joy awaited all who journeyed to Moody's Camp. When Dick and Lucile Seitz bought the camp from the Moodys in 1955, they carried on the treasured traditions that Ted and Myrtle had created.

On went the scrumptious American meal plan—served on white linen tablecloths with wildflower centerpieces—that would rival a five-star restaurant; the bounteous Sunday Swedish smorgasbord with tables laden with a symphony of foods including lutefisk, ham, rice pudding, and an endless array of mouthwatering salads and desserts; the hearty Saturday night prime rib dinner that welcomed arriving guests after a wearying day of travel; the Friday night fish dinner that, unlike the fish fry of today, boasted fried shrimp or butter-drenched lobster tail.

On went the Wednesday night square dances with their joyful music; the highly successful fishing guide services; and the

Lucile and Dick Seitz present one of their fine Sunday smorgasbords at Moody's Camp, circa 1950s.

Courtesy of Dick Seitz

Saturday noon cookouts that sent the smoky scent of burgers on the fieldstone grill wafting through the woods and across the water, drawing salivating guests in from the lake and forest to picnic tables bedecked in red-checked cloths and topped with enough potato salad, deviled eggs, baked beans, and chocolate cake to feed an army.

And on went the same personal service that guaranteed guests a restful or adventurous stay, depending on each individual's desires.

Only thirty-two years old when he made the leap from engineer at an Ohio firm to Northwoods resort owner, Dick Seitz, along with his beautiful wife, Lucile, brought an energetic youthfulness to the camp. Dick possessed a serene demeanor, while Lucile, who my grandmother Clara thought looked exactly like the actress Rita Hayworth, added a dash of glamour with her good looks and engaging smile. Together they made the perfect Northwoods hosts.

No one would have guessed they were novices.

When Dick heard about Moody's from a coworker who frequently vacationed there, he and Lucile decided to check it out. It was the fall of 1954. Shortly thereafter, they learned Moody's was for sale.

"We had been looking at several properties in the Hayward area," Dick explained. "But Moody's came closest to what we wanted." They took the bait.

"We found it all very appealing, especially the musky fishing. We thought we could run the resort and just musky fish at our leisure," he continued. "It didn't work out that way."

Leaving Ohio with no regrets, the Seitzes blew into the resort business on the blustering winds of March along with their three young children, Sharon, eleven, Kay, eight, and Doug, five. With only two months to learn the ropes before the forest floor exchanged its melting snows for carpets of white trillium and the first fishermen of musky season arrived, they plunged in.

"I had no knowledge of running a resort," Dick admitted.

Their guests and the private cabin owners who tapped into their services and hospitality would never know it. The Seitzes seamlessly transferred their gifts of organization, efficiency, and

charm to the already successful establishment that the Moodys had created.

There was only one major tradition that Lucile nixed early on.

"She switched Ted's T-bones for the Wednesday night steak fry to New York strip steaks because she thought there was too much waste," Dick explained. "She and Ted had a falling out over it."

Even though Ted had agreed to help out with the transition that first year, Dick said the steak dispute put a wedge between them, and the Seitzes were mostly on their own.

It didn't matter. Like all the other obstacles they would encounter in running a resort, the Seitzes were up to the challenge. To all who knew them, it seemed there was nothing Dick and Lucile couldn't do.

Did you want to fish? Dick made sure the bait tanks were stocked, sold fishing gear and licenses from the corner office, and arranged for guide service.

Did you want to go canoeing down the Namekagon River? Lucile packed a scrumptious picnic fit for royalty drifting down the Nile: fresh sandwiches; sweet, dribble-down-the-chin peaches; hard-boiled eggs; homemade chocolate chip cookie bars; and thermoses filled with cold lemonade went along for the ride.

Need a pickup from the overnight train coming in from Chicago to the Stanberry train station 25 miles away at 5:00 a.m.? No problem. Long before the train's early morning whistle announced its approach, Dick was there waiting in the camp's station wagon. You could count on it.

No matter the need, Dick and Lucile met it with a graciousness that camouflaged the myriad responsibilities already on their to-do list. Top of that list was to create a haven of delight for all who visited, and a lot of times that involved carrying on through the unexpected.

"When we had big storms, the power would go out, which meant there was no cooking or water available," Dick said. "And sometimes guests would let me know late at night that there were bats flying around in the cabins, and I had to attend to that."

Despite the surprises, Dick and Lucile kept the camp running efficiently for their guests. In addition, they were often on call for the unanticipated needs of the neighboring private cabin owners. Take, for example, the phone call Dick received late one night from a saloon in the town of Winter.

It was Woody, my mother.

When our car broke down on one of our twelve-hour driving odysseys to the cabin, my mother, alone at the wheel, knew exactly whom to call.

Stranded with the five of us kids ages twelve through two plus a sixteen-year-old babysitter, Woody politely refused the offer of several of the bar's patrons to drive us in their separate cars to our cabin more than 30 miles away. Unwilling to split us up, she called Dick instead.

"Woody, what are you doing in Winter at this time of night?" he asked in sleepy amazement.

It was his only response. He assured her he'd be there as soon as he could.

Under the curious stares of the barstool strangers, we kids waited in the saloon's smoky darkness quietly playing cards in a sticky booth to hide our unease. Thankfully, within the hour Dick was there. A man of few words, he calmly heaved the luggage of seven people from our station wagon into his. By the time we had stashed all the necessities that the backend could hold and squished all eight of us into the remaining space, it was well past midnight. Riding sleepily on each other's laps down dark forest roads, we silently gave a prayer of deep thanks for the familiar face of our rescuer. With Dick at the wheel, we knew we were safe.

Of course, mixed in with all these unforeseen events were the on-going chores of the camp's daily maintenance. When it was cold, Dick kept fires—the only heat for the lodge—burning continuously in the lodge's two fireplaces. When it rained, which it frequently did, he saw to the huge chore of bailing the camp's fifteen wooden Hayward-made Peterson Brothers boats. They either had to be bailed by hand using an old coffee can or dragged, waterlogged, onto a sling-type harness, cranked up, and then flipped over to dump the water out.

When the hot sun shone, he patiently pulled an endless slew of excited kids behind the camp's 35-horsepower ski boat down to the end of the lake and back for the bargain fee of a dollar a ride.

And for the fishing guests, of whom there were plenty, he saw to it daily that the boats and motors were always in top-notch running condition.

"Every spring the boats had to be painted," Dick explained. "We then sank them in the lake to make them swell so they wouldn't leak.

"We started out with 3½-horsepower motors, eventually upgraded to 5 horsepower, and finally ended up with 7½ horsepower, which was considered a big motor at the time."

In between these duties, he oversaw the camp's office, selling an assortment of candy, pop, beer, bait, resort gear, and fishing licenses; managed the resort's billing accounts; and attended to the maintenance of the buildings and grounds.

Although Lucile had some experience in the restaurant business, she had her hands full running the kitchen and overseeing a staff that included a main cook, a pastry cook, four waitresses, an office person who subbed as a hostess, and one or two chore boys.

In addition, she arranged for the cleaning of the thirteen cabins, oversaw the laundry, and on Wednesday nights did the cooking herself.

Supplies had to be constantly replenished: meats ordered from Sylas Products, dairy goods purchased from the Russell Creamery Dairy, and fresh produce fetched from Hayward farmers.

Help was often hard to find and keep. All three Seitz children joined in the work; Sharon and Kay, young as they were, waitressed from day one, announcing the daily specials and taking all orders from memory. Doug filled in as chore boy—his signal being two rings from the kitchen's cast-iron bell—doing miscellaneous jobs that included swatting at lodge bats with a badminton racket for a nickel per success.

Lucile hired college girls or local Ojibwe girls to clean the cabins but frequently found herself short of help. Late one summer, when desperate, she even approached my sister Nancy and me, then seventeen and fourteen, to fill in for a three-week stint. We jumped at the chance. Dick often had to take over the cleaning in the fall when the college girls went back to school.

With no rest for the weary, the Seitzes kept this ongoing service and hospitality running from March to mid-October, when the last of the musky fishermen headed home.

"We just hoped the pipes didn't freeze before the season's end," Dick said.

Over various falls and winters, Dick built a number of additions to the lodge, including the screened-in-porch and the dining room buffets. Every spring, he tapped trees on Sugar Bush Lane and boiled the sap over an open fire in a big cast-iron cooker down to more than 60 gallons of maple syrup.

It's no wonder that with the combination of such an elegant Northwoods setting and the Seitzes's gracious service and engaging personalities, the resort boasted a return rate of 85 percent. At the height of the season, the Seitzes were serving one hundred people dinner every night.

Despite such success, running a resort was not a huge moneymaker.

For $12.50 a day or $84 a week per person, guests received

Dick and Lucile's Wednesday noon cookouts prepared over the fieldstone fireplace by the resort's tennis courts were among the highlights of the summer in the 1950s and '60s.

Courtesy of Dick Seitz

a daily cabin cleaning, three outstanding meals, and laundry services. Boats rented for $1 a day; $3 included the gas and oil.

"I could have made more money in war bonds," Dick concluded.

✕

Looking back, it should have come as no surprise that such a workload over a twelve-year period would eventually become overwhelming. In addition to the resort work, during the 1960s Dick and Lucile took on the running of the Telemark ski shop in the winter, with duties that included flying to New York as buyers.

"It all got to be too much," Dick said. "We were operating thirteen months a year doing double duty, and then Lucile had a heart attack."

Yet, no one could have predicted the news that greeted us on that sunny spring morning in 1967 as we exited our church in Aurora, Illinois.

"Did you hear the Seitzes sold the resort?" asked Vera and Franklin Hobart, my parents' lifelong friends whose family cabin was on Big Spider Lake as well.

I felt like a wave of cold water had just slapped me in the face. How could that be? What happened? Who bought it? We all were shocked beyond words.

Never in our wildest imagination had we envisioned that the Seitzes would ever leave. They were the embodiment of all that resort owners should be: consistent, loyal, kind, good, dependable, and, most especially, fun. Beyond the great fishing, the beautiful scenery, the wonderful meals, it was their friendship that made the resort the paradise it was.

In my mind's eye, it is still one of those unexpected moments in time that are never forgotten. And even though I was only seventeen, I knew instinctively it would never be the same.

And it wasn't.

Although the new owners were kind and pleasant, they quickly altered the resort to fit their purposes. Early on, they changed from the all-inclusive American Plan cabins with meals in the lodge to housekeeping with a modified American Plan, thus giving guests options and thereby ending the daily gatherings of everyone for fine meals in the pine-festooned dining room. Ended also were the happy square dances that brought lake friends and families together in joyous camaraderie. Gone, too, was the availability of many other services that had been graciously extended to guests and neighboring private cabin owners.

But much more unsettling than the disappearance of the meals, the hospitality, or the amenities was the sorrowful scattering of friendships. Like a prize musky on a fishing line that suddenly breaks free, in a nanosecond, the resort's unique sense of community was lost.

Before long, the resort was sold again, and the new owners made the severing of the bonds complete by gradually selling off the cabins as condos.

Perhaps all of this was inevitable, part of what would eventually be the trend for almost all the chain of Spider Lake resorts. With the introduction of Disney World, family cruise ships, and attainable airfare to exotic locals such as Hawaii, a Northwoods resort for many may have begun to seem too antiquated. But for those of us who lived it, nothing could have been finer than the elegant simplicity of a woodland camp scented with the musty fragrance of forest. For the Seitzes, who made each journey there feel like a ride on a shooting star, it was heaven.

How we wished the charming hand-painted sign that hung over the dining room buffet and greeted guests with its daily reminder, "Here there is no time," were true. If, only for a moment, we could hear the music of the camp again: the clatter of the kitchen dishes, the enticing aroma of dinner cooking, the cheerful greetings of friends in the lodge, the melodious ring of the chore boys' bell, and the sweet strains of an accordion drifting through the night.

But just like the loveliness of Dick and Lucile's square dance waltz, it ended all too soon.

The Lodge Beckons

1923–1967

*"This is happiness; to be dissolved into something
complete and great."*
—Willa Cather

It was the heart of the camp.

Low slung, dark and rambling, its inner sanctum beat with
a life of its own, supplying all who entered with renewal, rest,
laughter, reflection, and camaraderie.

It was the perfect gathering place.

On damp, rainy days, it was filled with cozy chatter: the crimson glow of the fire dispelling the gloomy weather and offering
warmth and light for the knitters, readers, and card players who
circled its massive stone fireplace.

On sunny days, the cool shadows of the log walls offered a
quiet respite from the hustle of lake activities as guests passed
through to the office in search of a new lure, a cold Coke, or a
letter from home.

Three times a day, its dining room was a cacophony of cheerful
voices, fabulous food, and gracious greetings as resort workers,
guests, and visiting lake neighbors joined in equal friendship, regaling each other with their latest tale of adventure.

And on square dance nights, no place was finer. Music, light,
and laughter pulsated out of its walls and windows. It had a certain
magnetism, and we were drawn to it as if it were the North Star.

It was the axis around which its thirteen guest cabins and
neighboring private cabins revolved. It was the lodge. And anytime
we had a chance to go there, we went.

The Lodge, Circa 1959

"I need a loaf of bread and some milk," our mother announced. "Who wants to go to the lodge to get it?"

"I will!" we answered at once.

"Why don't you pick up some eggs, too," she added.

Thinking quickly, we four older siblings suggested we all go together in order to share such a delicate load. Thinking just as quickly, our mother, amazed at such sudden harmony and seizing the moment for some much needed quiet with just baby Mary, agreed.

There were no errand grumblings from this crowd, for something memorable was sure to be happening at the lodge, and we were eager to discover the drama of the day.

Would a gleaming fresh musky hang in huge grandeur from the garden's hook and scale? Could we sneak into the bait house to peek at the minnows and black leeches swirling in the cold, gurgling water of the tin tanks? Or would the log icehouse be unlatched so we could climb upon the mounds of sawdust and feel the cool breath of last winter's lake ice upon our faces?

It mattered not whether the action was subtle or sublime theater: we were never disappointed.

In a flash, we were on our way. Forgetting our mother's golden rule, such was our excitement, we let the back door slam. Its loud clap echoed through the woods like an encore and, thankfully, muffled our mother's scolding.

We were off!

Up our log-and-fieldstone steps we scrambled, the delicate sweep of maidenhair fern brushing our legs like a spider's touch, the cascading myrtle rippling over the log rises like a waterfall.

At the top of our gravel driveway, we pondered our first decision. Which route to take? The "low road" with its gentle curve and deep gravel ruts offering a view of the swamp and a glimpse at the dancing light of the not-too-distant thoroughfare? The secretive, seldom used "high road" with its shoulder-high banks dotted with mossy rocks and the opportunity to perhaps capture a horny toad or surprise a giant-footed snowshoe rabbit? Or maybe the wooded path past the four resort cabins on the hill, where opportunities for voyeurism into the lives of the current guests awaited us?

One of us became the leader by pulling in a favorite direction, and the anticipation of our adventure squashed any sibling squabbling that might normally have ensued.

Walking quietly together, we took in the details of our hike: scattered clusters of swaying purple phlox; the rosy insides of chipped and cracked granite rocks sparkling in the sunshine; patches of emerald moss silky soft to the touch; the curvy crevices of tree roots, where surely, our imaginations told us, elves and fairies lived.

Meandering down these slopes, we came to the rising hill of the camp. Like young deer pausing in the shadows to watch and wonder what was ahead, we slowed our collective gait and canvassed the scene. Seeing no one on the tennis courts or picnicking by the fieldstone grill, we raced each other to the rope swing hanging in the still shade of an oak's towering branches, just begging for a ride on its well-worn wooden seat.

The first one there took a running start, sweeping the swing into a graceful, long, deep arch. With a sibling pushing hard, the swinger rode up into the sunlit blue air like a dragonfly on a wind current, our hearts silently singing the old Robert Louis Stevenson poem our mother had taught us: "How do you like to go up in a swing, / Up in the air so blue? / Oh, I do think it the pleasantest thing, / Ever a child can do!"

Up, up, up the rider rose. Higher than the fieldstone grill, higher than the lodge roof, higher, or so it seemed, than the tree-tops. Then back down again for another rising loop with shutter-speed glimpses of the shimmering lake beyond.

"Push harder!" the swinger ordered to offset a sibling's lacka-daisical effort. "I want to go higher!"

When each of us had taken a turn, and we were dizzy with descent and fatigued with pushing, we wobbled away to the allure of our errand at hand.

The lodge beckoned.

Walking along the circular driveway, we quietly passed by the lodge kitchen, the hub of the resort. Here the signature scent of the daily cooking wafted through the screened windows. The sounds of clattering pans, soft voices, and quiet laughter drifted out from within like the cozy hum of a happy beehive.

Self-consciously, we wondered who might be watching us from the big kitchen table. Adorned with a blue-and-white-checked oil-cloth, a smattering of coffee cups, and a few well-used ashtrays, the kitchen table was a welcomed spot for the resort's fishing guides, cooks, chore boys, cabin girls, and owners Dick and Lucile Seitz to sit and take a break.

Glancing up at the cast-iron bell hanging over the door, we were grateful to be newly arrived and to know that it would be a while yet before the bell's heavy timbre would ring its mournful farewell. For when it tolled for thee, it was as sad as a loon's lone-some call on an empty lake.

But most of the time, the bell's joyous ring reverberated through the woods and out onto the lake announcing meal times, celebrating newly caught fish, and signaling for chore boys with their individually numbered rings to come running.

Rounding the corner, we were greeted by a sunny garden en-circling a tall log post, its huge hook and fish scale buzzing with the blue iridescence of sunlit flies just waiting for the next big catch to arrive. Dainty yellow butterflies danced amid the orange Turk's-cap lilies like partners executing a snappy square dance, allemande left.

"Hi, there!" came a friendly voice from behind, startling us out of our botanical reverie.

Tommy Seehuetter, one of the resort's fishing guides, was just exiting the bait house with a bucket full of minnows in one hand and a slew of fishing poles in the other.

"Hi Tommy!" we called as we watched his tall, trim figure stride down the path to a waiting client at the lake.

Furtively, we glanced around to see if Eddie the Guide was in the vicinity. With his tilted triangular cap shading his eyes, a gun on his hip, and a knife in his boot, Eddie's swaggering walk and silent charisma always created for us an intimidating aura of mystery.

But he wasn't around. Or at least we didn't see him. We moved on to the lodge's main entrance with its hand-painted "Ted Moody's Camp" sign hung to the side and hurried to enter its cool, dim shadows.

Swinging open the large screen door, we entered what seemed like an enchanted aerie.

Moody's lodge living area, circa 1950s and '60s, with its baby grand piano, fieldstone fireplace, and screened porch, provided a delightful place for guests to gather.

Courtesy of Dick Seitz

On cool, rainy days, we pushed a second door, a heavy wooden one, open as well, and walked into the golden glow of a crackling fire dancing in the massive fieldstone fireplace. Its cozy light and warmth fanned out to the handful of guests sequestered there on comfy sofas and chairs.

But on hot, sunny days, guests were mostly down at the lake or out fishing, and we had the place all to ourselves. Those were the best.

Tiptoeing in, we stood quietly for a moment to absorb the room's enticing atmosphere: the sprawling black bear stretched above the arched entry into the dining room; the antlered deer head over the fireplace mantle, its warm brown eyes seeming to greet us; the baby grand piano sitting regally in the corner waiting for a song; the mounted musky on the burnished log walls, its greenish gold scales zigzagging in the dim light as though it were still swimming in the deep darkness of the lake.

Although we were alone in this inner sanctum, the lodge seemed to emanate the love and laughter of all who had gathered there over the decades: it was as if we sensed the spirits of Ted and Myrtle, their guests, our grandparents Erle and Clara Oatman, and the many friends and families who had walked these floors before us. Blowing softly in from the porch, a gentle lake breeze swirled all the history and memories of the past together into a strong aura of peace and happiness.

Spellbound, we gradually moved under the wide, curved entrance cut through the log wall and into the dining room. In late afternoon, lake light filtered through the windows, casting the room in an amber glow. Rustic, white birchbark table legs stretched beneath linen tablecloths already neatly set for dinner. Centerpieces of wildflowers in hues of yellows, reds, and purples sparked the room with woodland ambience, and massive boughs of green balsam hung from the rafters, their piney fragrance suggesting Christmas had arrived early.

All was in readiness for the evening meal.

Scents drifted in from the kitchen, making our mouths water. We longed to come up for the scrumptious dinner and festive fellowship, but because our family of seven was an expensive lot to feed, those dining moments were reserved for special occasions such as my August birthday, the only one of our summer stay. It couldn't come soon enough.

As we enviously admired the preparations for the dining

Traditions at the lodge, pictured circa 1950s and '60s, included pine-bedecked beams, wildflower centerpieces, and delicious meals. The birch table legs contributed to the rustic elegance.

room's dinner, stuffed wildlife eyed us from all around the room: mounted muskies lined the walls; two stuffed loons—one in summer coat and one in winter—guarded the fireplace; a raccoon winked from a log rafter, and a skunk perched slyly in a corner. More rack-studded deer added to the decor.

Over the buffet hung our favorite sign: the clock with no hands that read, "Here there is no time." It only confirmed what we already knew to be fact in these magical Northwoods.

The "Here there is no time" clock, which sported no hands, hung in the lodge dining room, reminding guests to leave their troubles behind and enjoy all that the camp had to offer. Photo circa 1950s.

Courtesy of Dick Seitz

Checking the mail holder, we looked through the community pile for any letters to us: a sweet note from our grandmother Clara, a funny greeting from our father working back home, or a newsy note from a friend with the latest summer gossip.

"What can I do for you today?" came a voice from the kitchen doorway, once again shocking us out of our daydreams.

Appearing in his trademark crisp khakis and collared shirt, Dick Seitz, as usual, was on the scene, even attentive to the needs of four young children on an errand. Despite his busy resort agenda, he nevertheless waited patiently for one of us to gather our courage and speak.

"Our mother wants to know if you have an extra loaf of bread and some milk that we can buy," Nancy, as oldest, asked.

"I think we can see to that," Dick replied, looking us over with smiling amusement. "I'll be back in a minute."

Awaiting our goods, we studied the intriguing elements of the small office tucked at the back of the dining room. A vast selection of fishing poles; lures of every shape, color, and size, including Eddie the Guide's handmade "Eddie's Bait"; postcards; and a variety of sweatshirts emblazoned with *Moody's Camp* covered every inch of its walls.

But what really caught our attention was the glass-topped candy counter filled with chocolate Hershey bars, Juicy Fruit gum, Butterfingers, Snickers, Buns, and an array of other tempting choices. Anchoring the corner directly behind it squatted the square Coca Cola cooler, its red sides dripping cold beads of sweat; its slushy ice insides holding chilled brown-bottled Leinenkugel beer, Orange Crush, grape drink, root beer, Coke, and Dr Pepper.

As if this wasn't enough enticement, just around the corner beckoned an open-windowed ice cream bar brimming with choice-defying flavors: orange, raspberry, or lime sherbets; creamy vanilla; rich dark chocolate; and Nancy's exotic favorite, coffee.

Surely volunteering to help our mother, the arduous hike, and our well-behaved efforts warranted one of these treats?

Returning with the bread and milk, Dick set them on the counter.

"Anything else?" he asked with a grin, knowing full well what was coming next.

"I'll take a double-dip coffee ice cream cone," Nancy announced.

Encouraged by her bold lead, my brothers and I pounced.

"I'll take an Orange Crush," piped David.

"Make mine grape," added little Tom.

"And I'd like a Bun bar," I added.

"Please!" we each remembered at the last minute.

Smiling, Dick only nodded as he gathered up our requests one by one.

For, if the truth be known, this was our sibling secret. Baby Mary was out of luck.

"Charge it," Nancy said authoritatively.

Obligingly, Dick pulled out our running tab from the resort's wooden file account box on the counter and added our goodies, milk, and bread to its tally. (Our total bill at the end of our stay always surprised our father, such were the accumulations of our numerous "rewards.")

Savoring our treats, we drifted slowly back through the lodge once again and out into the summer's bright sunshine.

"Why, hello Oatmans!" Lucile called as she swung out the kitchen door. "How's everyone?"

With her slim figure attired in a chic shorts outfit and her dark hair framing her pretty, smiling face, one would never guess she was the supervisor of the kitchen activities, the help, the laundry, and the cleaning—all laborious camp duties.

"Fine!" we managed to mutter with our mouths full.

"Say hello to your mother for me," she answered, striding away.

"We will! Thank you!" we each answered, juggling our load of treats, mail, milk, and bread.

"See you at the square dance!" she said before disappearing into the steamy wisps emanating from the log laundry house across from the garden.

Choosing separate routes to devour our guilty pleasures, we nevertheless kept an eye on each other's progress, singing our father's favorite ditty to each other's bobbing heads: "I'll take the low road and you take the high road, and I'll get to Scotland before ye!"

Arriving back at the cabin, little Mary gave us envious looks. Unbeknownst to us, telltale signs of our treats stained our lips in faded shades of orange, brown, and grape.

Luckily, our mother was too busy to notice our transgressions. But she found others.

"Where are the eggs?" she asked.

Stunned, we looked at each other.

"We forgot," I said.

"Well, who will run back and get them?" she asked.

"I will!" came a chorus of voices.

In a flash, the back door slammed.

The Fishing Guides Cast Their Charms

1940s–1960s

"As the guiding went on, first friendships ripened into loyalties, and when old parties returned, the trips were always happy reunions."
—Sigurd F. Olson

They were men of mystery.

And they held the secrets to the lake. They knew the shallows, the reed beds, and the cold, deep pockets of the depths.

They knew the sky, too. The feathery wisps of cirrus clouds, the billows of cumulonimbus, the slight changes in wind, and the meaning of it all.

And they knew their fish—crappie, walleye, bass, and musky—what lure to use and where to catch them. They were men of the water. They were the fishing guides.

When the lodge bell jubilantly clanged, all knew these lake Houdinis had worked their magic once again, and many rushed up to the lodge's sturdy log pole set in the garden to see what magnificent fish now hung from its sunny scale.

Coming upon the guides as they strode from the gurgling bait tanks down to the boat dock, out to the lake, and back again with fish and beaming client in tow was like watching ongoing theater. With sparkling water as a stage and a bucket of minnows and a rod and a reel as props, no job to us seemed finer.

Tommy Seehuetter, Elmer Brunberg, and Eddie Ostling anchored the fishing services at Moody's Camp, and they were as different as individuals as the fish they caught. Their main

In the 1950s, Moody's Camp fishing guides often could be found down at the dock readying the wooden rowboats and 3½-horsepower motors for their next clients.

BIG SPIDER LAKE FROM MOODY'S CAMP HAYWARD, WISCONSIN T- 976

similarity was that they were men of few words, which only added to their rough, woodsy mystique.

Although their fishing attire usually resembled a similar uniform of clean khaki trousers, ironed shirts, and laced-up leather boots, they were distinguishable from a distance by their hats, which also matched their personalities.

Tall and lean, Tommy wore his brimmed cap at a jaunty angle that suggested his cheerful spirit and friendly disposition. Elmer's squat, sturdy frame was topped with a serious felt fedora that revealed his academic background as a teacher and principal. And Eddie's roguish rolled-edge hat pulled down low to one side over his eyes gave him the rugged allure of a James Dean–type maverick.

Sitting on our dock, it was easy to spot these guides on the lake by the silhouette of their hats. We watched as they tirelessly rowed across the water so a client could troll, motored their 3½-horsepower boats to another reed bed, or cast their own shimmering lines into the air like a spray of ice crystals on a hot day.

Yet, as glamorous as a career on the water appeared, the life of a guide wasn't easy. The pay was poor, the hours long, and, sometimes, the clients were ornery.

A Moody's guest weighs his fresh musky catch on the resort's scale, circa 1950s.

Courtesy of Dick Seitz

Tommy: Fisherman and Friend

Fishing and the polka were his passions.

And each was a dance that kept him on his toes all his life.

Born on February 6, 1925, in his family's Twin Lake home (the doctor had to borrow a Model T Ford and a pair of skis from the mailman to get there), Tommy Seehuetter credited his love of fishing to his parents.

"My mother and father went fishing every night," Tommy said. "If I hadn't been born in February, I'd have been born in a boat."

Seehuetter roots to the Big Spider Lake area go way back before his time. His grandfather Preston was a logger from the state of

Washington and came to Hayward during the great logging boom of the 1880s to open a steam-powered sawmill on what is now Murphy Boulevard and Preston/Lake Helene Road. According to Tommy, most of the logs used for the local cabins and resorts came from the swamps of North Lake and the north end of Big Spider.

Tommy reminisced that during his childhood, school was often called off because the roads were too muddy from logging and the runoff. "In the spring, we even had a mud week when the school closed down," Tommy explained. There were few roads in the area back then and no bridge over the North Lake thoroughfare to Moody's Camp.

In 1943, at the age of eighteen, Tommy joined the Navy (again, his love of water guided his life choices). He served during World War II until 1946, and eventually returned to Hayward, married Violet Leatrice Cline, and settled into the family home built over his grandfather's corner sawmill. There he and Violet raised six children.

Tommy worked a variety of jobs to support his family, including a stint as a sawyer. But it wasn't long before he was lured back to the lakes, casting his luck as a fishing guide on weekends, summers, and most anytime he could work it in.

"The first time I came to Moody's, it was by boat from Eggert's Resort across the lake," he said. "I also guided on Teal and Lost Land Lake."

In the early years when Ted Moody ran the camp, Tommy worked alongside other guides such as Hank Smith, an Ojibwe (locally known as "Hank the Indian"), Elmer Brunberg, and George Hewitt. The days started early and frequently ended late.

"They were often ten to twelve hour days," Tommy explained. "Sometimes I'd be out till 10:00 or 11:00 at night."

At Moody's Camp, it was Tommy's job to get the minnows and the suckers from the bait house, pick up a shore lunch that the cooks had assembled for him to fix over an open fire, and be sure the boat was bailed, gassed, and readied with oars and anchor.

Throw in the "pee can" (usually an old coffee tin), and he was set to go.

Then it was out on the lake for a day of fishing with clients.

"We went out in all kinds of weather," Tommy said. "The good thing was there were no mosquitoes on the lake."

The early motors were 3½ horsepower, so it took a long time to get from one fishing spot to the next.

"They didn't start very good either," Tommy said. "Sometimes it took two hours to get back, especially if we were out far, like on the Chippewa Flowage."

Most often, however, Tommy used the time-tested technique of trolling by oar. To the squeaky tune of the oar-lock rhythm, he spent hours rowing his client around the lake with a lure dragging behind the boat.

"We didn't have electric trolling motors, fish wells, or captain's seats like they do now," he said with a laugh.

It was all back work and muscle.

For lunch, Tommy would pull up to an island or shoreline clearing and gather wood to start a campfire.

"I always cooked a shore lunch of fried potatoes and any fish we had caught, which I also had to clean and fillet," Tommy explained. "Moody's always sent along some eggs to scramble just in case there were no fish."

Occasionally, in an attempt to fulfill his client's desires to catch that elusive musky, Tommy wound up performing chef duties well into the evening.

"Sometimes I'd be frying up steak and potatoes at 10:00 at night by car lights," Tommy said. "It wasn't an eight-to-five job."

To top it off, some of the fishermen didn't even know how to fish.

"I had a lot of clients that I had to teach how to cast," he said. "I learned to be a good ducker."

Many of the boats of that era were long, lean, low-riding wooden boats handmade by the Peterson Brothers of the Hayward area. Although heavy, they skimmed beautifully across the water for the rower because of their narrow design, unlike the wider hull of today's boats.

They were, however, tippy. Consequently, Tommy had one golden rule.

"I never let clients stand in the boat," he said. "If they wouldn't

sit, I'd say, 'See this oar? Do you want it on the side of your head?'

"You could drown if a client lost his balance and grabbed you or the boat and flipped it over."

Thankfully, most of Tommy's clients were well mannered and cooperative.

"Some clients griped a lot, but most did not," Tommy said. "Once, I had one complain so much because he was only getting weeds that I took him to shore and left him at the dock."

That client had to be one rotten fish for the kindly, gentle Tommy to take such a stand.

Most often, an outing proved successful, and the musky was prominently featured on Moody's menu that night. After a sparkling iridescent show on the garden hook for all to see, the fish was cooked, gussied up with garnish, and promenaded on a platter around the dining room by Ted Moody, and later by Dick Seitz, for all to ooh and ahh over.

Naturally, the proud fisherman regaled the admiring guests with tales of his conquest. An often-asked question was, "Who was the guide?"

Besides the musky, another frequent catch was the walleye. Too frequently, as it turns out.

"There were no limits on walleye back then," Tommy explained. "Some people hauled in as many as fifty to sixty a day. It was a dirty crime, and it hurt the lakes terribly."

Despite all the detailed personal services Tommy and other guides provided, the pay was low, especially for a father trying to feed six children.

"I was paid $10 a day, and the highest I got paid was $18 toward the end of my guiding around 1968," Tommy explained. "One client always gave me a dollar more for every fish caught over 30 inches.

"I liked fishing and being out on the lake," Tommy continued. "I would have liked it more if it had paid better."

Any of the day's catch not eaten were stored in Moody's icehouse in a hold above the sawdust-covered blocks of winter lake ice. Packed on a shelf on ice, they were reserved for the client to

Left: Tommy Seehuetter guided his client, Glen Zimmerman, to this 53½-inch, 35½-pound musky on Little Spider Lake on September 1, 1964.

Courtesy of Terry Seehuetter

hand carry or ship home—or saved for a private fish fry at the end of the client's stay.

Tommy said the biggest fish he caught were a 17½-inch crappie on Mud (later renamed Fawn) Lake and a 53½-inch, 35½-pound musky on Little Spider by the weed bed near the nuns' retreat. No wonder Tommy was such a popular guide.

He offered a few tips from his reservoir of knowledge. "When catching walleye, you have to let the bait bounce on the bottom like a crawfish," Tommy said. "Musky you have to just keep working at it and use spinners with different colors."

Although the clients drifted off after Labor Day, some of the best musky fishing continued on into October and November—although changing weather patterns added a few more challenges to the outing. "It would be freezing and there would be two inches of snow in the boat," Tommy said. "I'd catch the water from the back of the motor to warm my hands."

Whether he was frozen from whipping winds or sunburned and parched from a hot day on the water, Tommy headed home exhausted, ready to start all over the next day—but not before Ted Moody sent him off with a shot and beer to go.

In the off-fishing season, Tommy said he often guided during deer season and hunted regularly to feed his family as well.

"We ate a lot of ducks and deer," he said. "I started hunting when I was six and quit in 1997 at age seventy-two."

Tommy also was a caretaker for several nearby private cabins, putting in docks, opening and closing cabins, and helping with other miscellaneous jobs. One client even had him rake the woods in front of his cabin every spring.

"It was pointless," he said. "It took me over forty hours. He was a fussy old fart."

Tommy's reputation as a fishing guide was on par with his renown as a polka dancer. Come Wednesday nights when the lodge drew guests and lake residents for the weekly square dances, he and his wife, Violet, energetically swung into the first notes of every polka with the joy and dazzle of two butterflies.

Those on the dance floor had to be on collision look out, such was Tommy's polka zeal and zest as he and Violet circled the room. For those watching from the sidelines, Tommy's transformation from fishing guide to debonair dancer was as startling as the leap of a musky from a still, clear lake.

"The square dance was real nice because the resort people and the lake people and the workers all came together," Tommy said. "Those were fun days."

An understatement, if there ever was one.

><

When the Seitzes sold the resort in 1967, Tommy Seehuetter decided to leave soon after. An era had ended not only for the resort but for the fishing guides as well. Tommy, Elmer, and Eddie moved on to more secure work, for the guiding glory days, as they knew them, were over.

In the years that followed, it took a long while for those of us who love to watch the lake from our docks to get used to the emptiness that the guides' absent silhouettes created. In addition to the smooth glide of their boats and the gentle, rhythmic creaking of their oarlocks, we missed the sight of their hats.

For besides being great fishing guides, they were our friends. Strong, tough men you knew you could count on no matter what the need.

And so, their disappearance from the lake was as crushing as when a favorite lure flung into the wind unexpectedly breaks free. With a soft splash it drops out of sight, and, like a wave rolling by, leaves just the ripple of its memory.

Sometimes in the early light, when the rising sun and the morning mist are just right, it is as though we can see them still.

The outline of a jaunty hat, the contours of a sleek wooden boat, the sound of squeaking oarlocks, and the arc of a powerful cast float for a moment in miragelike splendor. But just like the mystic end of a good dream, we blink our eyes and realize all has changed.

Just the same, we tip our hats in silent salute.

Elmer and the Lost Fish, Circa 1961

It was not exactly a dream assignment.

Elmer the fishing guide must have wondered how the heck he was going to manage one woman, five kids ages four to fourteen,

My mother's circa 1961 fishing lesson excursion to No-Pi-Ming, a nearby private hunting and fishing club, provided, in the end, no actual fish—but it did give us an interesting fish tale, thanks to the best efforts of my brothers, David and Tom, and guide Elmer Brunberg.

two rowboats with oars only, a canoe, and a full day of fishing on a remote backwoods lake.

This was no hop-in-the-boat simple outing on Big Spider.

The red-haired lady's goal of the day was to take her clan back to No-Pi-Ming, a gated private hunting and fishing club with thirteen isolated, uninhabited lakes. Ted Moody, along with several others, had procured these approximately 4,000 acres of land in the early 1920s for their personal outdoor pleasures.

Even so, in the spirit of generosity of the times and under Dick Seitz's careful management, No-Pi-Ming allowed Moody's Camp guests and nearby neighbors fishing access for a small fee. Hiking to No-Pi-Ming's Eagle's Nest Lake the back way through a virgin forest and over old corduroy logging paths made of side by side horizontal logs was a free and favorite activity of many.

Our mother Woody believed, however, if you came to the Northwoods, you should learn how to fish. There was only one problem. We did not like to fish.

This did not discourage her. We were going to learn regardless.

And so she packed a picnic, life jackets, fishing poles, and, some-how, with our help, threw the canoe on top of the car. Merrily she rode us along over the bumpy, rain-rutted Lake Helene dirt road that led to the gates of No-Pi-Ming and on to Holmes Lake.

No complaining allowed.

Thankfully, the day was hot and sunny. Whether that meant good fishing or not mattered little to my sister Nancy and me. As teenage girls, we were only interested in getting a suntan, and we were plenty miffed that we were missing such a perfect day on the lake with our friends.

Putting on our best sulky moods, we slathered ourselves with baby oil mixed with iodine—the potent tanning potion of the times—and resigned ourselves to the day. At least the lake and the woods were beautiful.

We had been coming to No-Pi-Ming for as long as we could remember to picnic on the screened-in-porch of the property's rustic cabin. Without electricity or running water and just a few bare bunk beds and basic furnishings, we felt as adventuresome as Goldilocks visiting the cabin of the Three Bears.

That part we liked. To actually sit in a boat and fish all day was another story. My younger brothers David and Tom were prob-ably more enthusiastic than Nancy and I were, and our little sister Mary could happily amuse herself wherever she was. I'm sure our mother was ecstatic; another accomplished goal to check off her list.

Elmer's mindset was anyone's guess. A man of few words, he nevertheless greeted our fishing party with a warm smile and set to the task at hand. For the first shift, my mother assigned Nancy and me to one of the ribbed wooden boats with Elmer while she and Mary and the boys piled into the other boat.

With not much room to spare, we all gingerly climbed into our vessels and paddled out to different sections of the small lake.

Stuck with two surly teenage girls clad in the unlikely fishing attire of modest two-piece swimsuits, Elmer concentrated on pa-tiently threading our hooks with worms, setting the red-and-white bobbers, and waiting for the fish to bite.

And wait we did. Occasionally, our bobbers bobbed, but when hoisted out of the water, only the small remains of a mangled worm hung from the hook. The thought of out-of-control barbed lures flinging about his head must have caused Elmer to nix any casting lessons early on.

Sensing our lack of interest (he'd have to be blind to miss it), Elmer unwearyingly rethreaded our hooks (my sister and I definitely did not want to stab a gooey worm and get blood and guts on our hands), and the process repeated itself over the course of several hours.

No one spoke. As I mentioned, Elmer was a man of few words, and our mother had already warned us that noise scared away the fish. So Nancy and I, martyrs that we were, sat in stoic, stony silence. I can't remember having more fun.

In the meantime, our mother's boat was having more luck. A whoop and a holler and a flurry of movement indicated they had a fish on the line. We watched the commotion from our side of the lake as they pulled in one nice-sized bass after another.

Our mother had enough experience of her own to remove the hook and slide the fish onto a stringer that, for lack of a better place, she secured around the oarlock, which allowed the newly caught fish to swim alongside the boat.

Around midday, we broke for our picnic lunch back on the "Three Bears" porch, a pleasant spot to rest in the shade and enjoy the birdsong of the forest. But then it was back to our mother's agenda, and we regrouped for the afternoon outing. Nancy and I took Mary along with us in the canoe, glad to be relieved of our "learn-to-fish" duties.

Falsely assuring Mary that there was a worm on her line, we instructed her to watch the bobber while we basked in the sun and grumbled to each other about what our friends were probably doing back on Big Spider.

The second boat, immune to our hormonal pessimism, continued to haul in fish after fish. My mother was happy, my brothers were happy, and surely Elmer was happy, having freed himself from female teenage apathy.

In the late afternoon, our mother signaled for us to paddle in to shore. At last! I don't remember catching a single fish. The only thing I brought back was a sunburned back.

Still, we were curious how the others had done.

I'm paddling at No-Pi-Ming while my sister Mary attempts to catch a fish. Even with Elmer's good guiding, neither I nor Mary nor our sister Nancy (not pictured) had any luck fishing from our canoe.

"How many fish did you catch?" I hollered.

My brother reached over the side and hauled out a long, wet rope laced with dozens of good-sized fish on the stringer's white plastic hooks.

"We're set for an island picnic fish fry!" our mother said, beaming at her success.

I dared not ask who was going to clean them for fear of eliciting a new "goal."

Pulling up alongside the half-sunken wooden dock, we began to unload our gear, occasionally glancing down at the ghostly glimmer of the white stringer hanging from the oarlock with its numerous fish swimming in watery unison.

Everyone was in a merry mood, including my sister and me. Glancing up at the sun's slant, we figured there still might be time to catch a swim with our friends. The boys had some good fish stories to tell, and our mother surely was beginning to happily calculate an island fish fry guest list in her head. She knew these fish could feed a crowd.

Elmer, no doubt, was ready for a brown-bottled cold one.

Hurrying to make an exit and get back to our friends on the lake, we uncharacteristically, and without being asked, scrambled as fast as we could to haul up our gear. In minutes, the shore began to fill with our paraphernalia from the day: life jackets, fishing poles, bait buckets, oars, towels, and suntan lotion.

Each of us grabbed a load and started up the hill.

"Who's got the fish?" Elmer asked.

Suddenly, we all stopped and looked at one another.

As if on cue in a silent movie, our small fishing party made a sweeping slow-motion turn and looked back at the boat. The oars that had secured the stringer of fish to the gunnels lay tumbled on the shore. The oarlocks sat eerily empty, their sockets now naked.

Somewhere in the lake's murky depths swam a ghoulish cadre of fish strung together like some freakish Northwoods version of the Loch Ness monster.

A chorus of shock, disbelief, and "Oh, no's!" rang out like crows startled from a tree.

Even Nancy and I felt sorry for the fish. And because we had rapidly removed all the gear from the boat like a mass of swarming bees, no one knew or admitted to having grabbed the oars. Like the slippery backs of the fish on the stringer, the secret still rides in the deep, dark lake.

Elmer just shook his head.

Thankfully, like I said, he was a man of few words.

Eddie Calls the Shots, Circa 1963

No one messed with Eddie.

With a gun in his belt and a knife in his boot, he was the quintessential fishing guide. He was a man's man and a woman's man, and to us kids he was as fascinating as a character straight out of a *Hardy Boys* or *Nancy Drew* adventure book.

Lean and muscular, he walked with a sauntering strut that emanated a hint of cockiness. It was long before the days of macho gold chains, but he didn't need any. He was the real thing.

He wore his shirtsleeves rolled up, revealing sinewy forearms; he kept his shirt halfway unbuttoned, exposing a profusion of

Guide Eddie
Ostling, who often
sported a gun on
his belt and a knife
in his boot, strolls
past the lodge at
Moody's with his
fishing poles,
circa 1960s.

golden curls; and he tilted his hat at a rakish angle, shading his eyes from view, which only added to his mystery.

When he slipped on a pair of dark sunglasses, his rough, rugged persona of tough confidence was complete. The fact that he rarely spoke (at least to us kids) only furthered his mystique.

As a fishing guide, he was in high demand. He knew his stuff, and he wasn't afraid or intimidated by anyone or any situation.

When you fished with Eddie, you fished hard and long. Action and adventure were never far from his boat. Anyone who went out with him came back with a story to tell.

As a bachelor without the responsibilities of a family, Eddie stayed at the top of his game by continually testing the waters. When he wasn't guiding, we often spotted him from our dock, skimming slowly along in his boat as he peered over the side searching for signs of a new fishing spot.

Sometimes he'd be banked off an island, his powerful cast

Eddie Ostling, resort owners' son Doug Seitz, and a friend share a joke over their various catches, circa 1950s.

Courtesy of Dick Seitz

flinging water droplets into the sunlight as he tried out one of his original lures. Aptly named after himself, "Eddie's Bait," the most popular one, was heavy and huge with a series of sharp, three-pronged barbs that made strength a prerequisite to casting it. Any musky hooked on that thing was in trouble.

Frequently, he'd be down at Moody's long, L-shaped log boat dock casting away for hours to an exact spot time and time again.

He rarely missed. In fact, his casting precision was legendary.

One summer when I was fourteen, my best friend from home, Martha, and I were out on the lake paddling around in our green Grumman canoe. It was a blue-sky day and the lake was smooth as glass. We had spotted some friends down on the boat dock—a place where we kids often gathered to check out the day's action—and had canoed down to say hello.

Eddie was casting away and, as was his usual manner, just nodded his head in silent greeting.

Known as a teaser, he kept aiming his lure in our direction, where it dropped with a splash very near to our canoe. The kids and other adults on the dock were getting a kick out of how close his cast was landing without actually hitting us.

Each time the lure plopped down nearby, we let out a holler

of shocked surprise as a cold spray spewed over us. Everyone got a good laugh.

Thinking we would soon be drenched, we changed course, said goodbye to our friends, and began paddling across the beckoning waters. Chatting happily away, we had gone about 50 yards before we realized we were not making much progress.

Digging our paddles deeper into the water, we pulled harder. Oddly, especially since there were no big waves to overcome, we discovered we were going nowhere.

Puzzled, I asked Martha to put more oomph into her strokes. She swung in with gusto. We went nowhere.

"We must be stuck on something!" I said.

Although I knew we were in clear, deep water, I nevertheless peered over the side of the canoe to see if we had snagged a floating log or some mysterious boulder that I had not seen before.

From behind us erupted a burst of laughter. Turning around from my stern seat, I could immediately see that Eddie was the culprit. He was standing on the dock with the line of his fishing rod stretched tautly to the back of our canoe, having hooked his lure directly onto the canoe's stern sprocket.

Eddie had purposely snagged our canoe like one of his big muskies, such was the accuracy of his casting. No wonder he had been practicing so near to us!

To make our embarrassment complete, there was no way to become unhooked except to paddle backward until Eddie, with a mischievous grin on his face, set us free. Our escapade offered a new version of "catch and release," and I'm sure we provided quite a fish story at the kitchen table during the lodge dinner that night.

Juxtaposed to Eddie's competence as a fishing guide was his reputation as the caller for the legendary square dances at Moody's Camp. Holding court with a Leinenkugel as scepter, he anchored the band's corner of the dining-room-turned-dance-floor with kinglike authority. Without his trademark hat and sunglasses, a different Eddie persona emerged from his fishing guide guise.

With his now visible wavy blond hair combed neatly back, the knife and gun missing from his belt and boot, and a half-

Rain did not dampen the spirits of this successful 1955 musky outing for Lucile Seitz, guide Eddie Ostling, and a Moody's guest.

Courtesy of Dick Seitz

unbuttoned clean white shirt and pressed slacks as his attire, he suddenly transformed into a kind of sexy backwoods rock star.

Ruggedly handsome with penetrating eyes, he called out the words of each square dance with the same flair that he executed his fishing cast.

"Grab your partner and do-si-do!" he commanded, his articulation fast and smooth.

For one who was mostly taciturn in public, Eddie suddenly became a flowing fountain of words.

"Now duck for the oyster!" he sang as we swung through our paces. "Now duck for the clam!"

Eagerly following his orders, we danced to the commands of his clear, confident calls. Accurately and precisely, he ticked each movement off as our dancing feet followed with flying steps.

Everyone loved it when Eddie called. And whether you were on the dance floor or contentedly watching all the action from the sidelines, you were in for a good time.

For many, his contributions as a fishing guide, square dance caller, and jack-of-all-trades around the lodge added greatly to the charm and ambience of the resort community during those happy, heyday years.

But then, like the last dance of the night, the beauty of the show came to an end.

With the Seitzes selling the resort and the new owners ending the American meal plan, the curtained closed and the lights went out on many of the camp's traditions, including Eddie's many jobs. Different clients with different needs now filtered through the resort, and although Eddie continued to guide, he lacked the venue and exposure of the more structured resort days. Even the square dances were no more, sadly silencing his role as caller.

><

Over the years, we private cabin owners rarely saw Eddie again. As young adults, my siblings and I occasionally ran into him in the smoky haze of a local bar where he was holding court with other fishermen. But sadly, rumors of drinking problems, health issues, and other personal struggles replaced tales of his legendary guiding.

Late one August afternoon many years later, when the ending summer light paled to an amber glow in a faded aquamarine sky, I sat as a young mother at the end of our dock absorbing the lake's peaceful beauty while my three sons and husband played games up in the cabin. Somewhere off in the distance, the lone sound of a puttering motor on the otherwise empty lake caught my ear. It wasn't long before I spotted a familiar old wooden fishing boat motoring ever so slowly down the shore.

At first, I didn't think anything of it. Perhaps it was just some fisherman looking for a good spot to drop anchor. But then as I watched a little longer and the boat came closer, the silhouetted figure against the light began to take shape and the first thing I recognized was the hat.

Like a ghost emerging out of the hazy mist of the past, here came Eddie around the bend heading down our north shore. I blinked several times against the water's shimmering radiance, thinking perhaps I was mistaken as it had been years since his presence had dominated the lake.

But then, like Rip Van Winkle coming down from the mountain, he came more fully into view, and I knew it was Eddie.

Because it was late summer and the resorts were waning in existence, there was no other activity on the lake, and so it was easy for my attention to be focused on him. But more than that, I was fascinated by the pace of his boat. It moved along at the languid speed of a funeral dirge.

Oddly, Eddie was not looking down into the depths of the lake for a fishing hole as in days of old, but instead was gazing up at the north shoreline, studying each well-known cabin as he passed by as though remembering long-lost friends.

As he drew closer to our dock, I debated whether or not to acknowledge him for, having not seen him in years, I did not think he would recognize me as a young woman and, if the truth be known, he still intimidated me. Furthermore, rumor had it that his drinking problem had gotten significantly worse, and I wasn't sure what condition he was in. I wanted to remember the old Eddie.

Nevertheless, because he was so close to our dock, it was impossible not to acknowledge each other. As he cruised slowly by—his hat angled, his eyes screened by his sunglasses—he respectfully tipped his head in a silent hello and I waved a greeting back to him.

For a moment, time stood still and the past floated between us in a recognized tribute to an era gone by.

Then without breaking the cadence of his motor's sad song, he ever so slowly continued down the shore at a steady, snaillike pace. Passing by the haunts of his heyday, his gaze intent on the specter of all that had been Moody's Camp: the guest cabins on the hill, the lodge, the swimming beach, the sundeck roof capped with dwindling sunlight. Here, once upon a time, many a resort guest and lake friend had waved and called to him as though he were a returning Odysseus trailing a monster from the deep.

It seemed as if he were searching for and perhaps seeing all the familiar faces he had known over the years. At last, he passed the spot where the bustling boat dock had once been, its missing logs a final reminder that his days as king of its fishing arena were long gone.

The camp and all the private cabins along the north shore of the lake had been his home—the place where he had reigned as fishing guide, square dance caller, and friend to many. A life and times, like his own legend, now only a ghostly vapor riding on the wind.

As the sun went off our dock, the chill of the shadows replacing its warmth, I gathered my things to head up to join my family. With one last look, I glimpsed Eddie's boat continuing its slow tour, the sound of his motor fading into the distance like a lonely requiem, his gaze focused on the north bay shore's intimate details as though he were committing them to memory.

It was the last time I saw him.

Not long after, we heard Eddie was dead. He had collapsed in a tavern and died shortly thereafter. He was only in his mid-fifties. Ironically, much of the resort era of the Northwoods was also well on its way to its own slow demise.

Perhaps Eddie knew his days were numbered when he made that journey around the lake. And like the last cast of the day, it was his final farewell.

The Square Dance

A Song of Summer, Circa 1959

"Irene goodnight, Irene goodnight,
Goodnight Irene, goodnight Irene,
I'll see you in my dreams . . ."
—Huddie Ledbetter

We could sense the music before we could hear it.

Outside even the leaves of the woods rustled with anticipation. They swayed and whispered as though they were already sashaying to the songs to come.

Above them, the whole of the velvet, starry night pulsed with excitement.

Nothing, however, could surpass the flurry of activity inside our brightly lit log cabin as seven people whirled about its snug rooms making frantic last-minute preparations for the weekly Wednesday evening square dance at Moody's Camp lodge.

In the middle of the living room, our mother Woody stood poised over an ironing board, expertly pressing the wrinkles out of my sister Nancy's and my full-circled cotton skirts. Hot wisps of steam hissed upward like cumulonimbus clouds, engulfing her red hair in the already static atmosphere.

My sister and I battled for positions in front of the green metal dresser mirror as we combed and re-combed our hairdos. I plucked at the bow on my ponytail as she continued to sweep up the ends of her ducktail to get every hair in place. At ages nine and twelve, that was about all we could do for beautification.

Our brothers, David and Tom, ages seven and five, scurried about in the other small bedroom, tucking freshly pressed shirts into their Indian bead–belted corduroy pants. Two-year-old Mary wandered around contently, entertained by all the commotion as she waited to be attired in her soon-to-be-pressed ruffled dress, white anklets, and black patent-leather shoes.

Our father was just finishing up with a quick reshave over the bathroom's tiny enamel sink—which was a good thing, as there was a line to get in.

"Hurry up, Dad. I've got to go!" I yelled.

"Mom, is my skirt done yet?" asked Nancy. "I'm all ready!"

Suddenly, the first strains of a square dance song drifted over the woods and through the screens of our cabin windows.

"It's starting! It's starting!" We shouted in unison. "Hurry! It's time to go!"

Like a burst of firecrackers, we ricocheted around the cabin in all directions, searching madly for sweaters, flashlights, and stray shoes.

"Can we go? Can we go?" we begged.

"Yes," Woody said. "Take a flashlight and stay together. Dad and Mary and I will drive up shortly."

Before the count of three, the four of us were out the door.

Fearlessly, we headed into the dark night, surging up the rutted gravel driveway to the shortest route through the woods. Passing the three Moody's guest cabins on the hill, we noticed that their lights were all out and quickened our pace. We were already late.

Whoever held the flashlight led the way. The rest of us stumbled along, tripping over an occasional root or rock. We were too hurried to complain that the flashlight holder needed to share. And besides, we knew the wooded path by heart. The strains of the first dance pulled us onward like the entrancing music of the Pied Piper.

As we scampered up the hill and around the corner of the lodge, the laughter and golden glow of lights drew us ever closer to the square dance. The whole building was alive with radiant energy. Forgetting our usual shyness, we flung open the screen door and marched in.

Oh, what happiness greeted us!

Inside, people mingled from all around the lake: lodge guests, private cabin owners, the camp help, local neighbors, and even visitors from other resorts in various stages of activities filled the small rooms. On this summer evening, some gathered on the sofas for a cozy chat while children congregated in the porch's corner for a fast card game of Spoons.

But most filled the dining room, edging the dance floor in clustered chairs as they watched elated dancers swing through the paces of the "Virginia Reel."

With our best manners on display, we searched for an empty hickory-backed chair from which to view the action. Quickly taking our places, we drank in the scene swirling about us. Foremost was the Frank Jalowitz band, a three-piece combo usually consisting of an accordion, banjo, and drums. Although we children had heard the Chicago Symphony at Orchestra Hall, the square dance tunes could not have been finer. In our opinion, this was the music of angels.

Fascinated, we watched the accordion player squeeze his instrument back and forth with a gentle sway while simultaneously

Ted Moody poses with two members of the square dance band, circa early 1950s. Dances were held every Wednesday night at the lodge.

playing melody on the keys. The banjo player strummed his strings, and the drummer *tap-tap-tapped* a steady swishing beat.

But mostly it was the caller who mesmerized us all. Usually, it was fishing guide Eddie Ostling, who had miraculously metamorphosed into a debonair crooner. "Now allemande left! Now allemande right!" sang out his rarely heard voice in strong melodic dictation. You had to pay close attention to his calls so as not to make a fool of yourself. With giddy smiles, dancers moved through the set at a fast-clipped pace. Eddie was definitely the man of the hour. The stage was set.

Although watching the dancers was entertaining, our greatest need at the moment was to find a partner for ourselves. Anyone would do; we were not choosy. We were desperate. And since beggars can't be choosers, our dancing partners came in all ages, sizes, and sexes.

Doug Seitz spins his partner around the lodge's dining room dance floor while his lake buddy, Brian Wahl, watches from the sidelines, circa mid-1950s.

Courtesy of Dick Seitz

Because most of the dances required switching partners midstream through the many do-si-dos, you never knew who you might end up with. Sometimes a brother suddenly became the best friend he was meant to be; sometimes a dad took a gallant turn with his daughter; sometimes an unknown resort guest thirty years your senior did the honors; sometimes the handsome seventeen-year-old from down the shore and your shy ten-year-old self linked arms. Alas, you couldn't help but notice his brightening smile when the dance calls switched him over to the pretty sixteen-year-old resort waitress.

It mattered not, for eventually, there was at least one dance when everyone was lucky enough to land the partner of his or her choice. And then satisfaction shone in their eyes, in the clasp of their hands, and in the easy, light flow of their steps.

Those not dancing enjoyed the floor show while cheerfully entertaining each other: young mothers holding sleepy babies shared fond visits; fathers found old friends; elders eloquently held court; children played cards; and lovers strolled off for a kiss.

Woody and Pat Hines, the two young red-headed mothers of the crowd, sat side by side with their little daughters on their laps looking as flushed and vibrant as a Renoir painting. Our father sought out some of the older, longtime returning guests with whom he always enjoyed a conversation. Fishing guide Tommy Seehuetter and other resort workers mingled among the folks in close camaraderie, recounting the activities of the day. It mattered not what your day job was. In this small Northwoods community, all were equal, all were friends, and all danced with one another.

Eventually, the band took a break, and hot sweaty dancers stepped out into the cool, crisp night air. Smokers joined them, pulling out their cigarettes and exchanging fish stories between puffs, the glowing red butts gleaming in isolated darkness like the eyes of a wild animal. Within the lodge, men pooled together to tip back bottled beer. Ladies scooted their chairs over to chat as children scampered to the ice cream counter or into the office for a cold pop pulled icy wet from the slushy confines of the Coca-Cola cooler. Teenagers dealt a quick game of cards out on the breezy screened porch, cooling their amorous hearts, at least for the moment.

Occasionally, the hot, humid nights of summer forced the square dance outside to the tennis courts, where dancers swirled under the stars and the music rose with the moist mist. Revelers ringed the courts like they were at a Wimbledon match or sat at

On hot summer nights, like this one circa early 1960s, the weekly square dance was moved from the lodge dining room to the tennis courts for cooler dancing.

Courtesy of Bill Perrine

picnic tables to watch the action. Lit by the dim glow of torches, the dancing faces of friends moved in and out of the warm darkness as if they were woodland spirits playing in the moonlight.

But on this cool night, the dance was inside as usual, and when the band started tuning up again, guests returned faster than skittering crawdads on a sandy lake bottom. Eddie's suave voice beckoned dancers out on the floor yet again, and the night continued with renewed energy.

Not surprisingly, the Bunny Hop and the Hokey Pokey brought a full crowd, young and old, to the floor. Other tunes ensued as dancers moved through the paces, segueing easily from one song to the next with hardly a moment to catch one's breath. And as dancers continuously pulled new partners to the floor, an eclectic mix was always in motion.

Throughout the evening highlights rained like stardust from the sky: Tommy the fishing guide swinging his young wife, Violet, around the room with dazzling finesse in a fast-stepping polka; Eddie calling out the intricate moves like a stage actor delivering his lines with snappy allure; little children dancing with their parents; bashful teenagers sharing a first dance; and most lovely of all, resort owners Dick and Lucile Seitz waltzing alone to three-count elegance in a heart-melting embrace. No Broadway stage could have delivered more mesmerizing moments.

Little children loved square dance nights at the lodge as much as—or more than—the adults did. My little sister Mary, second from left, finds a friend to polka with, circa early 1960s.

And then, suddenly, it all came to and end.

When the band swung into the refrains of "Irene goodnight, Irene goodnight, / Goodnight Irene, goodnight Irene, / I'll see you in my dreams . . ." you knew it was over.

With panic in your heart, you searched for a ready partner, grabbed his or her hand, and frantically headed to the floor in a desperate effort to not miss the last dance. How could it have ended so soon? It seemed like it was only just getting started.

But without a doubt, the evening was coming to a close. The band smoothly transitioned from "Goodnight Irene" into "Goodnight ladies, goodnight gentlemen, goodnight ladies, we hate to see you go. Merrily we roll along, roll along, roll along, merrily we roll along over the bright blue sea. . . ."

It was then that you knew you had to wait a whole week to dance again. Or worse, if your vacation was over, your heart ached with the knowledge that it would be a whole long year before you might be lucky enough to return and relish such magic.

As the last note ended, a burst of laughter and clapping followed, hardly hiding the sorrowful sighs at the evening's closure. Friends bid each other fond farewells and headed home under starry skies. Those who came by boat maneuvered shadowy steps to the lake and, with the low rumbling start of their motors, set off across the waters under the breathtaking Milky Way.

Our family shuffled off to our station wagon parked amid the cluster of other cars by the camp's log garage. As the seven of us piled in and snapped on our seat belts, our suddenly sleepy selves watched quietly as our father swung the car down the narrow dirt road to our cabin. Only the sound of tires crunching on gravel filled the air as the headlights illuminated what seemed like an enchanted forest.

Circling into our driveway past our leaning log garage, we noted with satisfaction that a lovely lime Luna moth and a cluster of other colorful ones clung to its back door. Resting on the warm wood from their own spritely dance, they soaked up the heat from the overhead light like sunbathers on a dock.

Tumbling out of the car, we lined up in the cabin's dark hallway, waiting for our father to unlock the door. Then with quick goodnights, we stripped off our clothes, fumbled for our pajamas, and stumbled into beds, leaving our once freshly ironed skirts and shirts in a heap upon the floor. Gradually, the forest became still, the last boat motor quieted on a distant shore, and only the lapping waves sounded their rhythmic song. Slowly we began to drift off under their hypnotizing spell, as a reprise of square dance tunes swirled our hearts into exhausted, blissful sleep.

><

In my dreams, I can still see and hear those lodge night parties. But most of all I hear the music, its sweet, lyrical refrains echoing across the lake in suspended glory.

Dock Day Delight

1920s–1960s

"The lake is the landscape's most beautiful and expressive feature.
It is Earth's eye, looking into which the beholder measures
the depth of his own nature."
—Henry David Thoreau

Our dock danced.

It literally rocked with activity. From sunrise until 3:00 p.m., when the sun went off its end, we gathered there to swim, sunbathe, go boating, fish, visit, picnic, wade, and splash.

Just as it had been for my grandparent's generation, the dock was our mecca. It called us to the lake like a loon to its mate. From this stretched-out perch, we could sit for hours mesmerized by the cloud formations, the open sky, the stream of diamond-dancing sunshine on the water, or the frothy wind-whipped whitecaps rolling down the lake.

It was the first place we ran to after our arduous journey Up North, no matter how late the midnight hour. It was a constant gathering place for many of our friends. It was the place we sought for a quiet moment of solitude after a rainstorm, at dusk, or when the stars began to shine.

As for a calming sense of mind, nothing gave us more pleasure than to stare out at the water, the islands, the distant shore. It was our peace.

And that is why we loved it so.

For a child, no place could have been finer.

From our wooden pier we could observe our whole water and

Moody's Camp owner Lucile Seitz (third from right) enjoys a rare game of cards with several guests on the resort's popular swim dock, 1957.

Courtesy of Dick Seitz

woodland world because, best of all, everyone else was down at the dock, too.

There was handsome seventeen-year-old Jim Wedding skiing across the lake. There was Tommy the Guide, poles and bait bucket in hand, readying his wooden rower at Moody's boat dock for a fishing expedition. There were the Seitz kids, Sharon, Kay, and Doug, down at Moody's sandy shore along with a flock of guest kids frolicking in the shallows and pushing each other off the raft.

There was Eddie, anchored off the tip of an island casting his line side by side with a client. There were the Hobart girls, Jackie and Patty, floating on inner tubes off their cabin's shoreline. And there was the Perrines' caretaker and jack-of-all-trades, Al Wendy, expertly sailing their guests across the bay.

The entire lake was like a circus with a variety of ongoing acts. Sitting on the dock provided a ringside view. It's no wonder

With my grand-
mother Clara
swimming in the
background,
my grandfather
Erle Oatman
shares a story
with my mother,
seated on the dock
bench, during her
first visit to their
Northwoods home.

that when the sun shone and the sky was blue, no other activity beckoned to us more than spending all day on the dock.

Like most of the early-era docks of the 1920s and '30s, the one Erle and Clara had Ted Moody build was a narrow affair. Approximately four feet wide, made out of wood and painted turtle green, piers such as this one were basic, sturdy structures often anchored by a bench at the end. Here is where Clara took her morning swim, where Erle fished, and where my father zoomed off in his sporty green wooden speedboat with its jazzed-up silver motor. Here is where they called out greetings to the reclusive Hedley Jobbins on the next dock over or waved to friends rowing by in a boat.

It was all they needed: simple pier pleasures.

When we five Oatman children came along in the 1940s and '50s, the dock became our playground, our total entertainment for hours on end. We frolicked in the water until our toes and fingers were as wrinkled as worms; practiced swimming and perfecting our strokes; waded endlessly along the shore in search of frogs; collected half-buried clams for an impromptu artistic dock display; created and performed water ballet for anyone willing to

watch; and gathered sparkling stones from the sandy bottom as though they were jewels for a king.

There wasn't a single one of us (or most any other swimmer on the lake, for that matter) who didn't have a bit of green paint on the bottom of his or her swimsuit from sitting on a dock. It was a kind of Northwoods fashion statement.

As teenagers, sunbathing became my sister Nancy's and my main pursuit. We smeared our bodies from head to toe with a concoction of baby oil and iodine, and when our mother Woody wasn't looking, squirted lemon juice into our hair with the dim hope of becoming blonde bombshells. In our attempts at beauty, we looked and smelled more like garnish for a fish platter.

One of our best lake activities ever, however, was riding the "surfboard" our parents gave us for Christmas one year in the early 1960s. Basically, it was a slab of blue-, red-, and yellow-striped plywood connected by long hemp ropes to the back of our 1954 aluminum fishing boat. After a few well-placed pulls on our 7½-horsepower blue Evinrude motor, the engine roared to life like a lion, and we were off. Skimming across the water on this slippery surfboard, we felt like we were on a magic carpet ride. Even though our slow motor barely got us above the waterline, we felt like we were zipping around as fast as water bugs on a pond.

Amazingly, we older kids were allowed to run the boat for each other, and consequently found mischievous delight in dragging a screaming sibling over the weed beds at the north end of Big Spider. Our greatest horror was that we might fall off, get entangled in the slimy weeds, and have to touch the mucky, murky mud bottom where surely a slew of bloodsuckers awaited us.

Sometimes the driver slowed just for the sinking effect.

In addition to the surfboard, we found hours of hilarity by getting into the canoe with no paddles, pushing it off from the dock, and rocking it precariously back and forth from one side to the other until, after a moment of exhilarating suspense, it finally capsized. Out we'd fall into the lake laughing and screaming so hard that Woody had to hush us.

"Quiet down! Sound carries over water!" was one of her favorite mantras.

Unwilling to be squelched, we'd dive under the canoe and laugh ourselves silly in the huge air pockets underneath until our sides burst. Thankfully, from the canoe's swamped confines, our noise was muffled enough to spare the neighbors.

The dock was the launching pad for all our lake activities. Here is where we rigged the *Enterprise* and set sail. Here is where we piled into the canoe and paddled off to see the yellow, white, and purple hues of the water lilies; here is where we, ready to roam, loaded the rocking fishing boat for an island picnic lunch. And here, like an eagle returning to its nest, is where we contentedly headed home.

We napped in its pine-shaded sections, read on its warm planks, and chatted with friends who often stopped by for a visit but ended up staying for one of Woody's impromptu dock lunches: peanut butter and jelly sandwiches, tomato soup, and lemonade all carried down the forty-nine steps from the cabin on trays. No problem. The more on the dock, the merrier.

Despite all the activity, our rustic dock lasted for years and years. Occasionally, our father had to repair or replace a rotten board or jury-rig a section for added strength, but, more often than not, the dock was strong and steady. The main dock of our

From dawn until the sun went off our dock at 3:00 p.m., it was filled with activity. Here, my father, circa 1960s, keeps an eagle eye on all of our boating and swimming activities—including our favorite pastime of capsizing the canoe.

youth met its demise at my sixteenth birthday party after a throng of friends jumped off of it enough times that one end collapsed, thereby creating a slippery slide into the lake—the perfect finale for a teenage party.

With that dock's collapse, Woody grabbed the opportunity and did away with tradition. After all, with five kids, who had time to paint a dock?

She designed a masterpiece that served us for the next thirty-three years. Made out of redwood, the new dock's seven sections were six feet by six feet and as heavy as a loaded log truck when putting it in and taking it out of the lake. Long metal pipes sledge-hammered through dock brackets into the lake's bottom kept it secure. But Woody wanted the dock wide enough so that two people could easily sit side by side for a good visit and not have to move every time a child scooted by for a flying cannonball off the deep end. Her vision worked.

Our dock became an even bigger gathering place.

One of the things that made it so was the well-known fact that it boasted a perfect swimming area, a sandy bottom for those who

Our dock fre-
quently welcomed
a host of friends
and family for
sunbathing and
visiting, as seen
in this photo from
the 1960s.

wanted to wade, very few weeds to navigate, and a gradual incline
into deep water that made any swimmer feel safe.

Lake friends in need of an activity always knew they could find
something going on down at the Oatman dock. Sometimes they
floated down the shore in an inner tube; sometimes they buzzed
by in a boat for a quick chat; sometimes they walked the rustic
path that skirted the lake; and sometimes they hollered down from
the cabin and descended the steps with towel in hand. All were
welcome.

And when my parents' lifelong college friends, the Deeters,
Mellingers, and Allisons, vacationed next door in Moody's cabins for several summers in a row, our dock became headquarters
for four families. There was enough sunning, swimming, fishing,
boating, and visiting from its planks that it resembled an aircraft
carrier.

Water-safety rules, however, dominated all activities. Woody ran a tight summer ship, and we were never allowed to swim without an adult present. In addition, we always had to wait an hour after eating before we could go in the water, based on the then current belief that we could get cramps and drown. Violations meant lake privileges were rescinded, and who wanted that?

Launching ourselves from the sturdy confines of our dock, we tested our own personal waters: swimming back and forth between the neighbor's dock to reach a numbered goal; creating intricate water ballets; daring ourselves to dive deeper; making up new water games to entertain each other; setting sail in high winds; meeting the challenge to swim to the island and back; and, most illuminating, bravely opening our eyes underwater to discover the blurry beauty of silent sunbeams shining into the shadows.

For creative, intellectual, social, or spiritual growth, there was no place finer than our dock.

The docks are empty now.

No one seems to hang out on them anymore. And rarely does one hear the pipe-pounding melody of docks being put in that once echoed around the lake like the sweet notes of a calliope. Instead, in the spring they are rolled in on wheels and in the fall they are rolled out with hardly a sitter or a swimmer in between. Most are narrow, metal structures and are side-saddled with boat lifts that look like long-armed monsters. The seamless shoreline ringed with low, unobtrusive green docks has disappeared. Except for the fishing and boating activities, one can look around the lake and hardly see a soul enjoying the simple pleasures of the dock.

Have our senses become so dulled by the instantaneous flash of the technological age that the cloud patterns of the sky, the flight of an eagle, or the dive of a loon cannot hold our attention? Have we become so desensitized to the wonder of nature's detail that we do not notice or appreciate the iridescent beauty of a dragonfly's wings on a warm dock or hear the joy-jump-splash of a fish?

I hope not.

For if I were to have my choice of chairs in heaven, the dock is where you'd find me. In fact, when I sit on the dock and watch the sun rise, or follow the sweep of cloud patterns across a blue

sky, or catch sight of stars shooting through the Milky Way, I feel like I am already there.

A touch of green paint on my swimsuit bottom would just add to the glory.

The joys of summer in the Northwoods: Here I am, circa late 1950s, leaping off our dock in a flying cannonball with my best toe-pointed form, aiming for a huge splash in Big Spider Lake.

Bring on the Rain

1950s–1960s

"I am not afraid of storms, for I am learning to sail my own ship."
—Louisa May Alcott

We woke to stillness.

Snuggled in our cabin beds, we could see that the early morning light was somehow different. And then we heard it. A muffled rumble over the forest like drums beating in the distance.

My sister Nancy and I lay still just to be sure. And then, there it was again. Thunder.

With it came the first gentle pit-pat-pit-pat of rain on the roof like the tender tap of a soft-shoe dancer. We burrowed under our covers and listened through the screens to the symphony of sounds slowly unwinding all around us.

Boom! A new and nearer blast rolled down the length of the lake in a series of undulating baritone waves. Big, beautiful, and boisterous. Again the thunder came, echoing over and over itself like the crescendo of many timpani.

Suddenly, the storm was upon us, and the heavens broke forth with rivers of rain. It poured down the gutters in wild waterfalls; it slithered snakelike down the steps to the lake; and it cunningly found its way through a maze of shingles, tarpaper, and pine boards to the single tiny crack over my head.

The first drop on my forehead made me blink in disbelief; the second startled me out of my reverie; and the third sent me leaping out of bed faster than a jackrabbit to grab the kitchen dishpan in hopes of keeping my bed dry.

Yet even with the advent of a rainy day upon us, all in the cabin stirred with sleepy happiness.

One would hardly think this would be the case with a family of seven stuffed in our two-bedroom cabin. But no shut-in storm was going to dampen our spirits during our precious summer sojourn to the woods. In fact, we welcomed a rainy day with open arms.

Who cared if we couldn't lollygag on the dock all day, swim, canoe, or sail? We needed a break from the sun anyway. For despite the downpour outside and, of course, with no TV or even a phone to fall back on, we nevertheless knew activities and adventure awaited us. Our day was only limited by what creative options we could dream up.

Cabin fever was not in our vocabulary.

The first order of the day was to build a fire. Besides taking the dampness out of the air, its light and warmth bounced off the golden logs like rays of indoor sunshine keeping the outdoor grayness at bay.

The second order was to decide what to do, thereby creating a quandary only because there were so many choices. Out from the corner chest came a collection of games with varying attributes to debate: Would it be Candyland, Parcheesi, Monopoly, checkers, or card games of Hearts, Go Fish, or Spoons? Should there be a tournament? Or would a one-on-one match of Solitaire do?

The possibilities were endless. For the non–game lover, the choices were equally enticing: curl up in a corner with a good book while the game action played out before you; pick up some knitting and relax to its rhythm; or bake up some cookies, giving the cabin a double shot of sugary scents and sweet warmth.

For those with a creative heart, a rainy day turned the cabin into a perfect art studio: pull out the tin box of water colors with its six bright hues all lined up in a row and paint the pine-studded island offshore; grab the crayons and a pad of paper to master ballerinas, horses, or clowns; create little people out of wooden clothespins by painting on faces, cutting scraps of cloth to make clothes, and gluing on acorn hats.

For those willing to brave the rain, pie-pan gardens beckoned.

This meant throwing on slickers and heading out into the wet woods in search of spiky moss, sparkling rocks, pinecones, ferns, and twigs. Rain-washed faces and soggy shoes only added to the

Cooking a special treat was a favorite activity on rainy days at the cabin. In this circa 1954 scene, the scent of popcorn fills the cabin as my father, my sister Nancy, and I keep a close eye on the vintage popper.

fun. Back inside the warm cabin, we assembled our collection into tin pie pans, making miniature landscapes that were perfect for the clothespin people to reside in, thereby creating endless hours of imaginative play.

When those activities waned, outings to town, the Laundromat, a walk through the rain to a friend's cabin, or a stroll through the dripping woods to check out the action around the hearth at Moody's lodge became enticing adventures.

When we were really energized, turtle racing ruled supreme.

It didn't take much to persuade one of our parents to drive us and our lake friends or visiting guests out to old forest roads that wound past wild lakes and swamps to search for painted turtles. Packed in the station wagon, we hung our heads out the windows into the foggy drizzle, looking for turtles nestled in the long, wet grass or scrunched up in the sand beside the road.

Once we had five or six loaded in a box, we headed back to the cabin. The rug was rolled back, the furniture pushed to the side, and a finish line established at the end of the room by the fireplace. Then each contestant picked out a turtle, taped or painted a number on its back, and lined up his or her racer at the floorboard starting line.

A designated official called out, "On your mark, get set, go!" and the racers let his or her turtle loose.

Pandemonium ensued.

Some turtles scampered off, their claws clicking wildly on the waxed wood floor. Others smartly chose to just duck their heads back in their shells and not move an inch, thank you very much.

Hooting and hollering encouragement to our turtles, we rivaled fans watching the Green Bay Packers versus the Chicago Bears. After a series of hilarious races, the victor was presented with a homemade ribbon made by one of the artists, and the turtles, no doubt grateful, were returned to the quiet of the forest.

At some point during our rainy day activities, just like the turtles, each of us turned into his or her own shells of refuge.

Our longtime friends, the Allison family, join us for rainy day fun—including games, art projects, and reading—in our cabin, circa late 1950s.

Someone might head to the porch for a nap under an old pea green
army blanket, the rain creating a lullaby on the roof; another might
sit close to the fire and write a letter home to a friend; someone
else might burrow down on the log-framed couch to read; another
might choose to just putter and putz about in the coziness of the
cabin.

There came a moment, however, when each of us wandered
out into the cool, damp mist of the porch and simply sat still to
watch the splendor of the storm. Curled up in a blanket or heavy
sweater on our protected porch perch, we marveled at the lightning streaks cracking the dark sky with silvery brilliance. We
watched in wonder as the trees whipped back and forth as though
performing a synchronized dance; we studied the swirling patterns on the water as the wind brushed and stroked its surface;
but mostly we simply stared out in quiet reverie as the rain poured
down around us.

And then, subtly as though some elfin spirit had lifted a heavy

Our porch at Wake
Robin provides
a cozy spot for
watching a rain-
storm, circa
1950s or '60s.

curtain, there came a change. The rain lessened to a soft drip upon the leaves, the thunder faded, the wind turned to a gentle caress.

Suddenly, there it was: a shaft of sunlight breaking through the trees like stage lights on a dark set.

"I wonder if there is a rainbow?" our mother mused.

And with that, we bolted out of the cabin, down the slippery log steps, and out to the end of the dock as the last of the raindrops sprinkled down on us like a baptism from above.

Luckily, we were often greeted by a dazzling rainbow curving over the northeastern end of the lake, straddling wetlands, forest, and water in one majestic arch. Hues of purple, red, green, and gold shone against the pewter puffiness of retreating storm clouds.

In that silent moment, we all sensed we had been given a gift—not only in the rainbow but in the storm: the chance to be together, to use our imaginations, to seek solitude, to share, to get to know ourselves and each other better, and, perhaps foremost, to witness the wild beauty of a raging storm gradually turn to luminous light.

Cabin Girls Catch the Cleaning Spirit

1964

"Cleanliness and order are not matters of instinct; they are matters of education, and like most great things—mathematics and classics—you must cultivate a taste for them."
—Benjamin Disraeli

We hated to clean.

It was the last thing on earth my sister Nancy and I wanted to do. As teenage girls, we had other things on our minds: boys, hair, suntans, our figures, and our friends, to name a few.

In fact, our mother's frequent requests for my sister and me to dust or sweep or wash dishes were answered by as many whining excuses as we could think of in order to avoid such drudgery.

So no one was more surprised than the two of us to find ourselves cleaning cabins at Moody's Camp. And it was the square dance, of all places, that led us to it.

><

The night was damp and hot.

Dancers were swinging their way through yet another set of Eddie the Guide's fast-paced do-si-dos out on the tennis courts where the band had set up in the hope that a fresh lake breeze might offer a respite.

Taking a break from the action, I sat on a nearby picnic bench soaking in the scene, when, suddenly, out of the dim light appeared Lucile Seitz. Swishing toward us in her lovely white square dance dress with its full skirt and scooped neck, she looked as captivating as the snowy owls we occasionally glimpsed sailing through the forest.

Smiling warmly, she greeted my mother Woody, and the two engaged in a happy visit. Because I was sitting so close, of course I couldn't help but eavesdrop.

"I want to ask a favor," Lucile said. "I've unexpectedly had my two cabin girls quit. Do you think Nancy and Marnie would be interested in the job for a couple weeks, just to tide us over?"

My heart skipped a beat.

"I would think they'd be glad to," Woody said. "I'll ask them."

"It's so difficult to find help, and the camp is full," Lucile continued. "But I know this is your vacation, so talk it over with the girls and let me know."

What was there to discuss? I thought I'd died and gone to heaven.

Nancy did too when she heard the news. Dick and Lucile wanted us to work for them? We'd get to hang out with other resort workers in the kitchen? They'd even pay us to do this?

Like a musky leaping high and fast out of the water after a coveted mayfly, we jumped at the chance.

Two days later as a golden sunrise burst through the feathery fronds of the forest, Nancy and I rolled out from the warmth of our porch beds, hopped into our blue jean cutoffs and cotton blouses, and reported for duty.

I was fourteen and Nancy seventeen. It was the first job for both of us, and I don't think either of us knew the work that awaited us.

Walking quietly down the damp, dewy path of the woods that morning, we were filled with nervous excitement. We had no idea want to expect, but even at 6:30, we were ready and we were eager.

As we approached the kitchen confines, laughter, chatter, and clattering dishes echoed out through the screened windows. Sweet scents of cinnamon dough baking and bacon grease frying fanned out into the driveway.

We were as anxious as two skittish fawns. After all, the kitchen was the hub of the camp. It was where all the resort workers, who we so admired and who worked so hard to make everyone's stay so enjoyable, took their private moments to eat, rest, or relax. It was their respected personal domain.

Although we were hesitant to intrude, we were eager to enter their inner sanctum and see what it was like. And so our curiosity and enthusiasm for this new adventure propelled us forward. Nancy gingerly opened the kitchen's screen door and I stepped meekly in behind her.

Summer fun on the dock with our friends ended when my sister Nancy (second from left) and I (second from right) took on a three-week stint in 1964 as Moody's cabin cleaning girls.

Friendly greetings rang out immediately, putting us at ease. But I was so mesmerized by the sights and sounds around me that I could hardly move. Around the large table covered in blue-checkered oilcloth sat several of the camp's help, including fishing guides Eddie and Tommy, who were both savoring a last cigarette and cup of coffee before hooking up with their morning clients and heading out to the lake.

Dick stood up and welcomed us into the fold while Lucile fetched two place settings and insisted we sit down and join them for some oatmeal and a glass of orange juice before we got started. In our hurry to rise so early and be on time, we had neglected to eat breakfast and were more than willing to take her up on her offer.

Within minutes steaming bowls of oatmeal were placed before us, and we were encouraged to help ourselves to the brown sugar and a pitcher of cream. Shyly, we reached for both. As we later discovered, it was just the nourishment needed for the work ahead.

Eating quietly, we discreetly listened to the morning conversations: special requests from guests, outings planned, supplies to replenish, activities for the day. All the help seated round the table dished out their own stories and reports along with a lot of playful jostling.

Right: This long stairway of log steps led up from the resort's beach to one of the Moody's Camp cabins we cleaned. In order to get to the other side of the camp and to the next cabin, we often carried our supplies up and down this staircase.

Franklin and Vera Hobart Collection

We were amazed to find ourselves included in this revered entourage. We felt as if we had just taken our places in a royal court.

But like the Knights of the Round Table, duties called, and one by one, each worker left to pursue his or her agenda for the day. Dick set us up with our cleaning supplies, and Lucile explained the detailed routine for cleaning each cabin.

It seemed simple enough: sweep the floors, change the linens, clean the bathroom's sink, toilet, and shower, and wash up any used drinking glasses. There were thirteen cabins in all, and since the camp was full at this time of year, we had our work cut out for us.

At 7:00 a.m. when the breakfast bell rang, Lucile directed us to the first cabins vacated by families and fishermen seeking an early start to the day. As they sauntered into the sunny lodge dining room to the freshly cooked breakfast awaiting them, we scurried off to clean their cabins before they returned.

Awkwardly carrying our supplies of buckets, cleaners, and linens, we quickly figured out a routine. First, we changed the sheets and made the beds together. Then, while Nancy cleaned the bathroom (thankfully, by virtue of being older, she took on that important responsibility), I swept out the rooms and washed the glasses. Whoever got done first helped the other.

Because we often worked together at home doing dishes and other chores our mother assigned, we made a good team and

STAIRWAY AND CABIN AT MOODY'S CAMP
IS SPIDER LAKE HAYWARD WIS 3510700

worked fast. After all, despite the novelty of *working* at the resort, we didn't want to miss out on too much afternoon dock time with our friends. Naively, we figured we could do our job and swim and sunbathe, too.

With our first cabin successfully under our belts, we confidently moved on to the next, figuring that at our quick pace, we'd be done in no time. Loaded with clean sheets and towels, we bundled the used ones up and dropped them off between stops at the log laundry cabin, where steamy scents of bleach and soap billowed out in blasts of hot vapor.

It wasn't long before we realized that carrying the supplies and linens up and down the hilly woodland paths from cabin to cabin was just as much work as the cleaning. And it wasn't long after that, that the newness of the situation faded and our enthusiasm and energy began to wane. We got crabby. We got cranky.

"How many more cabins are left anyway?" I asked my sister, who had handled most of the details.

"We're only halfway through," she said. "We still have all the cabins on the hill up by ours to do yet. Remember, the camp is full."

She had to be kidding. But, of course, she was not. And, so, on we trudged. The energy of the morning quickly turned into fatigue, sore backs, and achy arms.

At last, we were finished. Dropping off our supplies back at the kitchen, we reported in to Dick and Lucile. It was close to 1:30 in the afternoon. They thanked us warmly, told us we'd done a fine job, and with satisfied smiles said they'd see us in the morning.

We dragged our weary selves back to our own cabin and, without even stopping for a late lunch, collapsed onto the saggy mattresses of our porch beds. Although we could hear our mother, siblings, and assorted friends having a gay old time splashing and swimming down at the dock, we were too exhausted to care.

Within minutes, we were snoozing like a couple of hibernating bears. By the time we woke up from our nap, the sun was off our dock. So much for lake time.

And so it went. Each day the same.

LAUNDRY ROOM - MOODY'S CAMP - 1963?

Three weeks of rise and shine at the crack of dawn. Three weeks of oatmeal breakfasts around the lodge's kitchen table. Three weeks of up and down hills carrying cleaning supplies to thirteen tousled cabins. And no matter how fast we attempted to hasten our routine, we never finished before 1:00 or 2:00.

I have not worked so physically hard since.

Yet, despite the labor involved, it was pleasant to enter the uniqueness of each little log cabin. Although small in structure, they boasted their own personalities along with varying views of the lake and woods. Fresh breezes from open windows or tiny porches helped keep us cool as we worked, and, for the most part, the guests were fairly neat, which made cleaning easier.

Our main drama as cabin girls arrived late one night when a family traveling up to the resort for their annual vacation hit a deer on one of the dark roads leading to the camp. To phrase it more accurately, the deer flew through the windshield and landed in the back seat on top of some of the family members.

When we showed up for duty early the next morning, the kitchen table buzzed with the accident's details. Dick and Lucile had attended to the family's every need and comfort during the

A small log cabin across from the lodge was the laundry washing facility for all the linens at Moody's Camp, circa early 1960s.

Franklin and Vera Hobart Collection

The Phyliss cabin, with its charming screened porch, was one of thirteen cabins cleaned daily by cabin girls.

Franklin and Vera Hobart Collection

middle of the night, even assisting with medical care. Fortunately, no one was seriously hurt.

As cabin girls, Nancy and I had to be constantly on the lookout for tiny shards of glass that continued to fall out of the family's clothes and belongings and onto the linens, floor, and furniture of their cabin throughout their two-week vacation. We never knew when we might be surprised by the sharp slivers as we cleaned their cabin, and so we performed our duties as if surrounded by poison ivy.

Despite the daily routine, a crispness soon filled the early morning air and before we knew it, the approach of Labor Day signaled that a new school year was about to start. It was time to head home. We turned in our cleaning supplies and Dick handed us an envelope of pay for our services.

"See if you think this is fair," he said.

Cautiously, Nancy and I peeked in our envelopes to discover a ninety-dollar check written out to each of us for our three weeks of work. Wow! That seemed like an awful lot of money. We were thrilled.

"Yes, that's fair!" Nancy said.

"Thank you so much!" I added, thinking of the new school clothes I could now buy.

Nevertheless, I can't say I was sad to see my cleaning job end. I missed those lazy dock days on the lake, my friends, and cabin time, not to mention that I was dog-tired. We had been trained well, thanks to Lucile's good instructions and Dick's supervision, and despite our dislike of cleaning, we put our hearts and souls into the tasks at hand. After all, we did not want to disappoint Dick and Lucile.

We would have even swum through weeds for them.

><

Nancy returned the following summer, after her high school graduation in 1965, with a friend to work as lodge waitresses. They lived over the camp's garage with another waitress, which sounded very fun and exotic to me. But my mother thought I was too young to stay with them unchaperoned and live that dream.

As luck would have it, just when I did become of age, the Seitzes sold the resort, and I never got my chance. I've been sorry ever since.

For despite the hard work and the early and long hours, being a cabin girl was a job I relished. What could be finer than to wake in the dawn's glorious light, walk through the woods with my sister beside me, and eat a bowl of oatmeal around a kitchen table with some of the finest people my young heart had ever known?

Besides learning to clean, I snagged a behind-the-scenes peek into everything that went into the maintenance of resort life as well. All my romantic notions of running a resort vanished faster than soap down a drain as I cleaned cabin after cabin, day after day.

For behind the easy grace, camaraderie, fine food, and excellent fishing that camp life provided, there swirled an endless display of physical labor and meticulous care to detail by some of the kindest, most honest, hardworking, and devoted folks I have ever met. Their seamless efforts made the camp a Northwoods delight for all who played and rested there.

To their credit, those continuous toils were the best-kept secret of the camp.

But mostly I recognized that I got a lucky break on that long-ago square dance night. Whenever I am asked what was my first job, I am pleased to respond.

"I was a cabin girl," I say. "I cleaned cabins at Moody's Camp, a Northwoods resort, when I was fourteen years old."

"Boy, that must have been hard work!" is the common response.

"Yes," I reply. "But it was one of the finest experiences of my life.

"It was an honor."

Born to a
Northwoods Birthday

August 15, 1949

"Think where man's glory most begins and ends,
And say my glory was I had such friends."
—William Butler Yeats

My birthday cakes sang of the forest.

No fat frosted roses circled the sides. No *Happy Birthday* in skinny script swirled across the top of a store-bought cake.

Instead, they were homemade rounds of angel food cake wreathed in a cloud of white frosting lightly laced with wildflowers, pine boughs, and ferns.

And when the loons sang their flight songs across a purple dusk as though contributing an accompaniment to the beloved voices of family and friends ringing out around me, their cherished faces backlit by candlelight, no finer gift could be granted.

For a Northwoods girl, being born in August was the icing on the cake.

✕

Perhaps because my very first birthday party took place amid the grandeur of the Northwoods, I have always wanted it so. And for the better part of sixty-two years, my wish has come true.

On August 15, 1950, my parents placed my one-year-old self snugly in my highchair outside amid the sheltering shade of pine, oak, and birch behind our cabin. As family and friends sang "Happy birthday to you . . ." my mother placed the beginning of what would be a long line of lovely wildflower cakes upon my tray.

1950   Myrtle and Ted Moody with Marnie Oleson

I, however, was more mesmerized by the pretty light of my single candle and promptly stuck my finger through its hot flame. It made for a good laugh over the years, and, thankfully, did not deter my curiosity for all things bright and beautiful, especially those of the Northwoods.

From a young age, I knew there was no better place to be than Up North. And lucky for me, our annual family vacations usually coincided with August 15. With a handful of exceptions, I've been able to celebrate my birthday in the Northwoods ever since; it is a gift that only multiples in significance with each passing year.

Although simple in nature, my birthdays have always been remarkable to me. Just to be surrounded by woods and water was a gift in itself. During my growing-up years in the 1950s and '60s, my main present was to be treated to dinner at Moody's lodge. My birthday was just the excuse for the whole family to enjoy an evening of fine dining and friends. Seated at one of the larger tables in the middle of the room, our family of seven savored this blissful ambience and the evening's sumptuous entrée.

But as the birthday girl, I dined in suspense.

For sooner or later, Ted or Myrtle, and later Dick or Lucile, waltzed my wildflower cake out of the kitchen, and when they did, it was as if the whole room glowed from the light of the little candles. Instantly, the cacophony stopped and family, friends, resort staff, and guests turned and sang to me. And in that birthday moment, I felt blessed beyond belief with friendship and love.

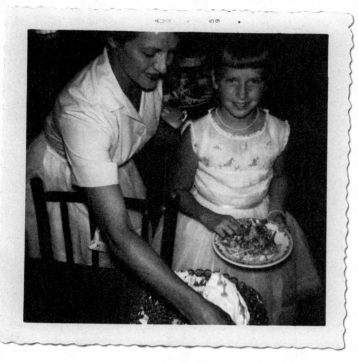

Lucile Seitz helps me serve my birthday cake during my tenth birthday party dinner at Moody's lodge, 1959.

My Northwoods presents, however, came with a flair entirely their own.

Back home, my girlfriends received dolls, pretty clothes, sweet perfume, fun jewelry, and other coveted feminine treasures for their birthdays. But not me.

I got fishhooks.

I cannot say that fish bait, especially for a girl who did not particularly like to fish, answered the heart of her desires. Although I politely acknowledged the wooden fishing lures' interesting colors and shapes—the bright orange and reds, the two-tone greens, the sparkling blacks—those big, barbed hooks were what really got my attention. And Eddie's Bait—designed and crafted by the charismatic guide himself and of which I received several—was the king in that category.

My sister Nancy had already lodged one of those sharp barbs in her head, such was our fishing finesse. So flinging one of those showstoppers around in the wind was not really at the top of my fun list. Yet, year after year, fishing lure birthday gifts accumulated to the extent that one might think I was striving to open up my own bait shop.

Unfortunately, most of those lovely lures, now of vintage value, were lost over the years by my siblings' and my repeated attempts to create our own fishing folklore. Flung out into the various weed beds of the lake where false rumors suggested the fish hung out, my lures, one by one, were snagged and snapped off forever.

The muskies must still be laughing.

One of the reasons I got so many lures is that it was difficult to go shopping in the woods. With Hayward more than 20 miles away, one did not exactly make a town run just for a birthday present. Consequently, family and friends simply headed up to Moody's to select a gift from the items that lined the walls and shelves of the lodge's office.

It was a one-stop shop.

So it was no surprise that, year after year, in addition to my abundant collection of fishing lures, I also received whole boxes of Hershey chocolate bars, packs of Spearmint and Juicy Fruit gum, a collection of red-and-white bobbers, an occasional Moody's Camp sweatshirt, and, on one memorable birthday, my very own musky rod.

I could have been a guide.

Despite myself, I loved that fishing pole. With its ivory shaft and red-wrapped trim, it had a kind of fishing femininity that spoke to me. Besides, even if I didn't like to fish, at least I could look the part.

Although it was a short rod, believe me, this was no kid's pole to catch minnows. Strong and sturdy, it was designed for heavy-duty action with a musky—a thought that sent shivers up my spine. After all, those monsters had fangs that would rival those of the wolf in "Little Red Riding Hood." Consequently, I looked upon that rod with reverence and respect.

I carried it around with love and devotion not only because it was my very own, but because it gave me credibility when I went for a boat ride even if I was just going out to cruise idly around the lake.

Ever appreciative of these gifts and the thoughts behind them, I did try to fish. I really did. But mostly I just unsnagged weeds from my hooks or endlessly, cast after cast, detangled the fishing line in the reel, which, for some unknown reason, constantly became a snarled mess that looked like Medusa's hair.

Alas, the only significant fish I ever caught was a 15-inch walleye whose eye I snagged while trolling off an island as a friend rowed me patiently along. It was a gruesome catch. Our artist neighbor, who was visiting from home, inked its lovely image onto a Big Spider Lake map. Tacked to the bedroom wall of the cabin it has hung lo these many years, a proud reminder of my big fish success story as a young girl.

My musky rod is one of my most treasured processions, a beloved birthday gift from my parents—beloved obviously not for the big musky I never caught but for their belief in me that I could.

><

Fortunately, in addition to these fine fishing-themed presents, there gratefully and literally appeared a silver lining: gifts from two men I loved dearly.

The first, from my father, was expected.

For years, his signature birthday present to each of my siblings and me was a stack of silver dollars to match our age. But as silver dollars suddenly began to rapidly disappear from circulation, he spent hours tracking them down from the dwindling supplies of various area banks.

So when I lifted his brown paper–wrapped present out of my fishing lure booty and felt its weight, I knew he'd done it once again. Tumbling the shiny silver coins into my lap and fingering their intricate design and long-ago dates, my father's thoughtfulness and love shone through more precious than silver.

The second silver gift, from resort owner Dick Seitz, was always a surprise.

Somewhere during my birthday evening at the lodge, usually

when I least expected it or when I thought he had forgotten me, Dick would appear out of nowhere and slyly slip a cool silver dollar into the warmth of my hand accompanied by a quiet "Happy Birthday, Marnie." Sometimes he'd surprise me in the dim glow of an outside square dance; sometimes in amid the dining room's merry sounds; or sometimes he'd appear out of the shadows by the kitchen's back door as we started our walk home.

I never knew if he did this for all the resort children who celebrated birthdays at the lodge or just for me. It matters not. All I know is that he never forgot. And like the gift of the silver dollar itself, his was a friendship you could count on.

⚊

It is my sixteenth birthday party that stands out the most in a long line of celebrations.

Maybe it was because in just a few short years the lake era as we had known it would end. Maybe it was because as teenagers, we were on the cusp of young adulthood, with all our desires and dreams before us as bright as a moonbeam path across the lake.

And maybe it was because it was just plain, riotous fun.

It wasn't just my party, however. It was a dual celebration for my childhood friend Patty Hobart and me thrown by my mother and her grandmother. With our birthdays just days apart, Patty's on August 12 and mine on the fifteenth, Woody decided a Sweet Sixteen party was in order for the two of us.

As was often the case, Patty was up at the lake at the same time as we were, staying at her grandparent's cabin down the shore. Never having celebrated our birthdays together before, Patty and I were thrilled at the prospect, and we happily came up with a guest list comprised of the young people we knew on the lake.

Our families over the years had shared an entwined history: Patty's grandfather, Arthur Hobart, and my grandfather, Erle Oatman, had been business partners in the Oatman Brothers Inc. dairy business; our fathers, Franklin and David, had grown up together; and our mothers, Vera and Woody, became loyal, lifelong friends from their earliest married days.

Most parties in the Northwoods were spontaneous and this one was no different. With just a few days to spare, Woody divided up the tasks and got the fun rolling. Patty's grandmother painstakingly made matching sugar cube corsages tied with pretty ribbons for each of us. Woody wrote out stylish invitations on birch bark gathered from the forest floor and sent my siblings off to hand deliver them, no doubt causing a posse of gift hunters to descend upon the lodge office. Business must have boomed.

Because it was a Sweet Sixteen party, there was much teasing about whether Patty and I had ever been kissed. There was obvious room for much speculation. Over the years on the lake together, we had both shared long-term crushes on our buddy Doug Seitz, who must have been in his glory when the two of us showed up at camp: two summer blondes tagging along beside him to fish, frog hunt, play cards, and swim. Patty and I were like a couple of eagles eyeing a catch.

If the truth be known, Patty was his hands-down favorite, and since handsome Jim Wedding across the lake was a few years too old and otherwise engaged with another lake beauty more his age, I accepted my losses like a guide cutting bait and set my sights on lake neighbor Brian Wahl. Unfortunately for me, he was more interested in driving his new ski boat. Who could compete with that? In unspoken agreement, however, neither Patty nor I owned up to the kissing question.

Since our cabin was the party place, my sister and I were assigned cleaning duties; as experienced cabin girls, sweeping and dusting were now our specialties. When those chores were completed, Woody sent us off to the woods to gather pine boughs to decorate the cabin windows.

On the day of the party, Patty's actual birthday, the sun shone warm, the sky beamed blue, and the dock was ready to dance. Our friends and siblings, ranging in age from eight to nineteen, arrived in a flurry of excitement, surging into our cabin's narrow hallway and spilling into the living room with swimsuits, towels, and an assortment of presents festooned with ferns and pinecones.

Sitting side by side surrounded by this circle of love and friendship, Patty and I opened our gifts, which—along with the obligatory fishhooks and bobbers—for once included some feminine treasures such as silver charms for our bracelets, tiny china forest critters for our collections, and even perfume from Lucile.

Sixteen must have been the magic number to finally nix the fishing theme.

After enjoying one of Woody's beautiful buffet lunches adorning the cabin's log table, we kids all charged down to the lake for the main attractions of the day: the swim party and games. Before we jumped in, our friends and siblings gathered around our cake on the dock and sang "Happy Birthday" to us as wind whipped our hair and sunshine warmed our backs. Turning sixteen couldn't have been sweeter.

Then it was on to the water games. The favorite was the watermelon seed–spitting contest orchestrated by Woody—an ironic choice from my very proper, etiquette-minded mother. Not only were we allowed to spit, we were encouraged to do so as far as we could.

Patty Hobart and I display our sugar-cube corsages at our joint sixteenth birthday party on our dock, 1965.

Shooting our seeds out into the lake in a long-distance competition, it wasn't long before all hell broke loose. Party decorum disappeared and major water shenanigans and horseplay quickly replaced any manners that were left.

We must have been crazed by sugar and hormones.

The old dock had never held so many jumping, hopping, scrambling kids before. We chased each other over the top in an effort to push and shove each other in; we linked hands in a long line and, in a resounding springboard bounce, leaped into the big waves like a spray of skipping stones. We jostled and splashed and dunked one another in a merry madness that bordered on a wild disregard for safety.

No doubt Woody tried to corral us, but none of us heard; her reprimands disappeared into the whoosh of waves and wind.

It didn't take long before the deep end of the dock began to sag. In a matter of seconds, after one heavy group bounce from its trusty boards, the two end sections collapsed into the lake and, as the white-capped waves washed over its planks, a perfect slippery slide was created.

It was pandemonium from there on out.

Like crazed otters, we threw each other and ourselves down the sloping dock, slamming into the water and onto swimmers below. Scrambling back up again, we took running starts, shooting ourselves feet first down our new runway. Woody quickly realized that saving the dock was a lost cause at this point and gave in to the fun.

There wasn't a kid in attendance who didn't go home with either a banged-up shin, a dock-painted swimsuit, or a splintered backside—party favors extraordinaire. When my father arrived a few days later, he could only stare at the dock's remains and mutely shake his head. But for Patty and me, our Northwoods Sweet Sixteen birthday party was a spectacular success.

><

Unbeknownst to us, it was our last hurrah.

Only a few years later, the resort was sold, birthday dinners at the lodge were no more, and friends grew up and moved on to college and careers.

Gratefully, I was able to continue my Northwoods birthday dinners with beloved family and lake friends on our cabin porch where, amazingly, my mother's wildflower cakes and even a surprise silver dollar or two from Dick Seitz blessed our gatherings together for more than four more decades.

It was not to be so for dear Patty.

Tragically, at only thirty-one-years-old, she was killed in a car crash out East, where she lived with her husband. Her parents, Franklin and Vera, received the shocking news in the early morning hours of their wedding anniversary. I last saw Patty on her wedding day, a talented and beautiful young woman filled with a sweet spirit of kindness and joy, happy and bright just like she was at our Sweet Sixteen birthday party, and beaming with the promise of all things stretching out before her.

Just a few years ago, when we were Up North together, Vera shared a tender story. After Patty's death, they had found among her treasured keepsakes her birchbark invitation from our Sweet Sixteen birthday party. It made me weep to think of it, but I was not surprised.

Mine still hangs on the cabin's living room wall, thumbtacked to a log. Whenever I look at it, I flash back to that day, the friendships and beauty of our youth epitomized by those joyful leaps off the dock.

For a birthday is not really about us, but about the life we have been given and the people who have graced it. To celebrate that gift with family and friends in the Northwoods amid forests, stars, lake, and sun is to recognize all the more one's blessings.

These days, on soft summer nights, my family and I often gather down at the dock to watch the heavens unfold. On those lucky evenings when a full moon, round and bright like a silver dollar, slides up from the silhouetted forest and into the evening sky, I am reminded of and eternally grateful for the circles of love and friendship that sustain and gift our lives.

And on Patty's birthday, August 12, when the annual Perseid showers peak and a myriad of shooting stars split the darkness with their fleeting splendor, the fragility and preciousness of life once again are underscored for me.

Romance in the Woods

A Summer Sweetheart Finally Arrives, 1965

*"How sweet the moonlight sleeps upon this bank! Here we will sit,
and let the sounds of music creep in our ears. Soft stillness and
the night become the touches of sweet harmony."*
—*Shakespeare*

Lucky for me he loved the lake.

Some do not, you know. Too many mosquitoes, too much rain,
too hot, too cold, too many flies and spiders and bears—oh, my!

But for those who love the Northwoods, no place is more
romantic. So, naturally, I longed to have my boyfriend Dave join
me for a week at the cabin. I'd given up snaring my guy friends
on the lake, and I was tired of watching my older sister and her
lake friends have all the fun. When my strict parents acquiesced
to my request to have my high school sweetheart come up for my
sixteenth birthday, I about fell off the dock.

Riding shotgun with your girlfriend's father for a nine-hour
drive Up North would not exactly be the desire of most recent
high school grads heading off to college in a few short weeks, but
this guy jumped at the chance. In fact, he drove most of the way
so my father could rest. I'll never know if it was the Northwoods
or my fifteen-year-old self, but the moment Dave arrived, he was
smitten.

More than his handsome green eyes, engaging smile, or lean
athletic build was the fact that he was funny and kind and sensitive. I couldn't wait to show him all that I loved about the lake.

He took to it like a fish to water.

Arriving in time for my Sweet Sixteen dinner party at the lodge,
Dave was immediately initiated into the epitome of Northwoods

ambience, fun, and friendship. From there on out, we hit the dock running.

We sunbathed and swam, sailed around the lake, canoed through the water lilies, hiked the road through the virgin forest to Eagle's Nest Lake, attended the Indian powwow in Hayward, walked to the bridge over the thoroughfare, picnicked on the islands, skied behind Dick Seitz's 35-horsepower ski boat, ran around with lake friends, toured the souvenir shops in town, dined on doughnuts and cold milk at the Lumberjack Hall in Hayward, and buzzed about in our 7½-horsepower fishing boat, almost always in the watchful company of family and friends.

Under such prying eyes, snatching a kiss became a problem.

Suggesting a 9:00 p.m. garbage run to the dump—a local hot spot for lovers—would have been slightly conspicuous. Going for a walk and clutching in the woods meant more mosquito swapping than kissing, and heading off for an early picnic breakfast on the

My then boyfriend and now husband Dave Mamminga drove up from Illinois with my father in time for my sixteenth birthday party dinner at Moody's lodge, 1965.

island, a rather creative solution if you ask me, was swiftly nixed by my mother at the moment of our departure. She insisted we could not go alone and sent along my little sister Mary who, like a diminutive spy, was often silently catching us in a cabin kiss anyway.

So much for romance.

Not to be thwarted, we asked permission for a date night at the outdoor movie theater in Hayward. With my father back in Illinois working, my mother seemed to think it was all right as long as we were home by my usual curfew of midnight.

We hit the road for the 20-mile trip to town in my grand-mother Clara's 1955 tank of a Buick—which my siblings and I had aptly christened the Big Black Bomb—under the August night sky, ecstatically happy at our freedom and crazy in love.

Parking amid the speakers that stood like sentries guarding the gravel field, we settled in for a night of popcorn and Cokes, and, of

Sailing on the *Enterprise* was one of the Wake Robin activities I introduced Dave to during his first visit in 1965.

course, a bit of innocent snuggling. Not surprisingly, neither one of us remembers the movie, but that was because the drama of the evening was yet to occur.

Actually, I think the film must have been fairly good because we do remember being disappointed that our curfew was fast approaching and we wouldn't be able to see the end. There was no point in hunting down a phone booth to call for permission to stay out later since the cabin had no phone, so we pushed our time limit to the max.

Finally, with the Buick's luminous green dial clicking closer to midnight and the 20-mile return trip looming, we knew we had to give it up. After all, being grounded was the penalty for missed curfews in our home, and who wanted to be grounded in the Northwoods?

Despite our best intentions, a missed curfew was the least of our problems.

Leaving the scattered lights of town behind, we sped out onto the darkness of the forested highway in an attempt to ease the severity of our lateness. We had not been on the road for long when the familiar *thump-thump-thump* of a flat tire accompanied the whistling wind through the windows. We could not believe our bad luck.

Were we in trouble now or what?

Carefully, Dave glided the car onto the weed-ridden shoulder, where it slumped to a halt. For a moment we sat in the intimate darkness we had longed for, but this was no time to kiss.

Out we hopped into the black night to survey the damage. We could barely see, yet it was obvious that the front left tire was flat as a pancake. With not a light in sight except the stars (my father's usual flashlight under the front seat having mysteriously disappeared) we set to work.

Actually, Dave set to work. Using the headlights to at least illuminate some of the shadowy night, we popped the trunk, pulled out the jack, and cranked up the mammoth old Buick as if she were a black beast rising out of a swamp for a nocturnal wandering.

My only job was to roll the spare tire to Dave when he was ready. Never adept at aiming, my misguided effort sent the tire sailing past him. In the light of the headlights, we watched in horror as it picked up speed, rolling and wobbling down the entire length of a long, steep hill until finally hitting a rock, ricocheting off the road, and slamming into a pine tree.

No movie could have had a better ending.

If an owl had been watching silently from a nearby treetop, he would have observed two teenagers laughing hysterically, stumbling down the road and, having retrieved the tire, stumbling back up, changing it bolt by bolt and nut by nut, and then roaring off down the road and over the hill at a high rate of speed.

"Whoo-whoo-whoo was that?" he surely sang out in the ensuing silence.

In the meantime, the clock in the old Buick was ticking away.

Because we were now really, really late, I suggested to Dave that he take what I thought was a shorter route to the cabin on one of the less frequented back roads. Not familiar with the way, he nevertheless kept his foot on the gas in order to keep me out of the hot water that I was no doubt surely in.

The headlights suddenly illuminated a hairpin curve to the left. Braking frantically to slow the Big Black Bomb, Dave spun the steering wheel hard to the left in an extreme effort to navigate the curve.

It was too late.

Like the orneriness of a fighting fish, the weight of the bulky Buick sent us careening in the opposite direction. In a flash, our speeding car flew off the road and slammed into a low embankment on the right. The impact threw us across the car seat, crushing our bodies against the right-side door.

It was not exactly the embrace we had been looking for.

For the second time that night, we sat in stunned silence, the clings and clangs of the Big Black Bomb echoing through the night as it lay on its side in the ditch. Shocked and stuck together by our entangled limbs, we could hardly move.

"Are you OK?" Dave asked.

"My arm and hip hurt from the door handle," I said. "But I think so. Are you?"

"I'm all right," he answered.

"Could you get off me then?" I snarled.

"I'm trying!" he answered.

There was no hysterical laughter this time around.

Suddenly like a scene out of Edgar Allen Poe, there came a tapping, a soft and gentle rapping, a *tap-tap-tapping* upon our now dusty and darkened door. Spooked beyond belief, we looked up from our upside-down view toward the window where the ghostly outline of a wide-brimmed hat peered down at us. Frozen in our entangled position, we could not have moved if we wanted to.

"Is everyone all right?" asked The Hat.

"We think so," Dave said as I looked on in wide-eyed terror.

"I heard a big bang from my farm just down the road and thought someone might have crashed," continued The Hat. "Came by to see if you needed help."

Amazed, we were stunned at how quickly our farmer friend had arrived on the scene. He must have moved faster than the speed of light, for it seemed to us that he was there within seconds of our sliding off the road. Struggling to untangle ourselves from our tilted angle, we gratefully thanked this midnight Samaritan for his offer to help push us out.

"Let's see if you can drive her out of the ditch first," The Hat suggested.

As though scaling a hill, Dave slid up the high slant of the seat to the driver's side. Putting the car in neutral, he carefully turned the key. The engine roared to life. Better yet, when he put the beast in gear, she rolled right out of the ditch. Daring not to stop now that the Big Black Bomb was actually moving down the road again, we honked to The Hat and a dark hand waved back. With no time to lose, we peeled away to resume our journey.

Rubbing my sore hip and arm, I glanced at the glowing clock-face with dread. Fast as the blink of a lightning bug, our curfew had come and gone long ago. It was now well past 1:30 in the morning. But our troubles on this oh-so-romantic date were not over yet.

My mother's wrath awaited.

At last, the Big Black Bomb crunched down the cabin's gravel driveway and came to a halt. In the faint glow of the back door light, we circled the car and surveyed the damage. Astonishingly, there was only a slight dent in the right front bumper and a few minor scratches on the side. Giddy with relief that the car and we had somehow survived the harrowing mishaps of the night, we quietly waltzed into the cabin's narrow hallway hoping my mother had gone to bed.

She had not.

Dressed in a black velvet robe, Woody sat rocking back and forth in the kitchen by the dim light of a kerosene lamp, her arms folded against her chest as though struggling to contain the anger within.

"Where-have-you-been?" she asked in a voice like chalk on a blackboard.

"You won't believe what happened!" I said as we greeted her.

By the looks of things, no, she probably would not.

Sincerely apologizing, we explained all the events of the night as best we could without bursting into laughter. Seemingly satisfied that we weren't "necking" in the woods all this time, Woody graciously forgave us and called it a night.

My father, however, said, "Not so fast."

A verbal explanation was not enough. When he heard the news back in Illinois of the flat tire and crash Up North, he ordered a typed report from me upon my return back home at summer's end, which was to include the answers to such questions as: "What was the name of the movie? When did it end? How fast was the car going? What were you doing on that stretch of the road?" And, my personal favorite, "Were both of the driver's hands on the wheel at the time of the crash?"

I believe it was my first effort at reporting—an interesting journalistic assignment if there ever was one. But I was so insulted by this "punishment" that I hammered away on the keys of my father's manual typewriter like a crazed detective on a deadline. All I needed was a cigarette and a hat. No report could have dripped with more sarcastic detail.

And, yes, the driver's hands were on the wheel!

Fortunately the facts of my "crime report" apparently won over my father, and the matter finally faded away. All that remained were the Big Black Bomb's dent and Dave.

Like I said, lucky for me he loved the lake. And so I married him.

One cabin honeymoon, three great sons, two lovely daughters-in-law, four precious granddaughters, one adorable grandson, and forty-seven summers on the lake later, I asked my husband of forty-two years what he loved most about that first visit. Without skipping a beat, he answered, "That you were there."

Dave and I share some teenage dreams on Big Spider Lake, 1965.

Like the flat tire on that long ago night, *thump-thump-thump* beats my happy heart.

Lake Lights

"For my part I know nothing with any certainty,
but the sight of the stars makes me dream."
—Vincent van Gogh

The lake is ringed in darkness.

No cabin lights twinkle from across the shore. No glaring garage spotlights fill the forest with their blinding fluorescence. Instead, only the trees' feathery branches are silhouetted against the starry sky.

For on this particular night, the electricity is out.

Feeling graced with this opportunity to view the lake in complete darkness, we make a beeline for the dock and settle ourselves upon its hard wooden planks now dry and wave scented. Our imaginations transport us back through the ages. Like sailors navigating by stars on the ancient seas, we look heavenward in awe and wonder.

Here before us is how the lake looked before it was settled. Here is what the Ojibwe saw as they camped along its shore. Here is God's creation as it was at the beginning of time in all its natural loveliness. Amazed by the grandeur, we gaze up at this same firmament and sense its sacredness.

Blinking and twinkling, a multitude of shining stars wink back at us from the black sphere above. The Milky Way cleaves the heavens with its flowing silver stream. A white crescent moon hangs low and pendulous in the western sky. So bright and strong are the constellations that their images float upon the smooth, dark lake, which serves as a mirror doubling their glory.

There flies a shooting star! And there another, following as though in a game of starlight tag.

Natural lake lights in their many forms have endlessly enchanted us.

Glorious golden sunrises and rosy red sunsets draw us to their splendor. In between, we dock dream for hours, staring out at glistening waters or up at the wisps of ever-changing cloud patterns swirling and floating like sailing ships in the blue above.

For us, sky watching brings a calming contentment like none other.

When sunlight breaks through the trees at storm's end, we dash to the dock to see if we can catch a rainbow. If we are lucky enough to be rewarded with an arch of pink, purple, and gold stretching over the retreating grayness of a storm-swept sky, we stand mesmerized.

When northern lights shoot their eerie green iridescence skyward in undulating waves, once again we stumble down dark steps to the shore and scan the horizon, captivated by this dance. Humbled by its brilliance, we become acutely aware of this gift of life that is so briefly, blessedly ours here on Earth.

Perhaps, however, it is the common, ordinary twilight that speaks to me the most.

Summer after summer, I have watched the end-of-the-day metamorphosis with welcoming anticipation, never tiring of its subtle beauty. As the red sun slips behind the darkening emerald treetops, there is a fleeting moment when pale pink dusk covers the sky like the inside sheen of a shell. Across the lake, the forest flares up golden like an angel's halo, glowing one last time before its light, too, begins to fade, and a grayish blue good-night washes the sky.

There comes with the twilight a quiet.

It descends softly over the forest; there is no rush or hurry. Gradually, almost imperceptibly, varying hues of deepening amethyst permeate the sky, luring one into a peaceful trance, a spiritual settling of the soul.

From the cabin's porch swing, I have swayed year after year across the decades, mesmerized by the twilight's shifting shades.

As a little girl swinging and reading in the dim light of kerosene lamps, I felt comfort with the changing luminance around me. As a young mother rocking, I rested in its glow, listening to the low, lilting voices of my three sons playing games with their father inside the cabin, their happiness echoing out to me in the dropping temperature of the night.

Wake Robin's porch swing, circa 1960s, offered a serene spot from which to watch twilight spread across the sky.

And now, as a grandmother gently gliding, the twilight wraps me in the warmth of tender memories, its radiance a reassuring bridge from the past to the future, as a new generation discovers the joy of lake lights.

Somewhere down the shoreline a soft laugh floats through the forest. A loon sings its love song, serenading the night.

Finally, the dusky purple twilight turns to black and a hushed silence fills the air. Through the treetops, a single silver star sparks the sky. One by one, others begin to join it, igniting the darkness with their twinkling glory and lighting the way to tomorrow's dawn.

Leaving the Lake

"The real significance of the wilderness is a cultural matter.
It is far more than hunting, fishing, hiking, canoeing.
It has to do with the human spirit."
—Sigurd F. Olson

It is quiet now.

Only the sound of lapping waves is left. They rock upon the shore soothingly, easing the loneliness that is as palpable as a heavy fog.

Where for days there was noisy laughter, there is now only calm. Where for hours there was continuous activity—swimming, boating, card playing—there is now only stillness. Where once there were endless meals on the make, there is now only a clean and tidy kitchen.

The sailboat is off its mooring, the sails wrapped and stored, the boats pulled up, the inner tubes put away, the dock chairs back on shore, the car packed.

Like a Tilt-A-Whirl at the fair, how the time together flew!

In a flurry of bell ringing, you sent off your loved ones one by one, and, now, the void that their leaving creates makes you want to weep. And sometimes you do.

Shortly, it will be time for you to leave as well, but, for a moment, you take a rest from your closing duties to glide on the porch swing, replaying the cherished memories of lake and cabin time that have ended all too soon.

In truth, sometimes amid all the commotion of being together, you longed for a peaceful moment. But now that it has come, your heartbeat hangs in the air, resonating like the last, lone note of a moving musical performance.

For you know the chance for another gathering will not be

repeated for some time, and, so, as if it were a reprise of a symphony, you replay and savor in your mind all that you experienced together. A loon's call is your accompaniment; the rhythmic ripples of a duck's wake your beat; the soft breeze your baton. The picnics, the parties, the friends, the swimming, the sunrises, the starlight blend in an encore.

For a moment, time stands still in solemn sacredness.

But now it is time for you to depart as well. Time to turn the key and lock the door and leave the loons to glide and the eagles to soar in uninterrupted tranquillity. It is their time for solitude.

You know that no matter how long the time until your return, whether it is weeks or months or even a year or more, it will always seem too distant. And when you finally do come back, turn the key, and walk into the cabin's welcoming mustiness, you know, feel, sense, as though the cabin is a living breathing thing that has been waiting for you, for love and happiness to fill its rooms once more. In that instant, it is as though two hearts beat as one.

But now it is time to go.

And so you say your farewells, glancing around at all that you hold dear: the gentle-eyed deer over the mantle, the green breadbox with its painted maiden, the fireplace hearth dusted with a filigree of ashes from the final fire, the faded hats of beloved earlier generations still hanging on the wall.

For a second, you imagine the cabin without you—the daylight and its shifting shadows, the hush of a purple twilight, the silver streams of moonlight—and you are filled with peace.

With a heavy sigh, you walk out the door and turn the key in the lock. The brilliance of a blue sky, the flickering sunlit leaves of the emerald forest, and the sparkling lake seem to engulf you with a parting embrace, for, often, no day is lovelier than the one on which you leave.

Abruptly, as if saying farewell, a loon's haunting call breaks the loneliness of departure. Another answers. Then all is still.

Till we meet again, dear cabin, I'll see you in my dreams.

Epilogue

"This little corner of the earth smiles to me beyond all others."
—Homer

Eighty-three years and five generations later, Wake Robin is still here.

Like the trillium, the lovely three-pointed-star wildflower for which it is named, our affection for this little log cabin in the woods blooms perennially.

But why? What is it that draws us back year after year? What is it that kindles our spirits and makes us long for it even in our dreams?

Why is it that we keep the same log furniture, antiques, blue Spode china, metal beds, and kerosene lamps that our grandmother Clara picked out in 1929? Why don't we switch out the 1950s fishing poles suspended from hooks that line the living room wall, the battered copper teakettle, the faded braided-wool rugs?

What is it about the green breadbox stashed with nuts, nails, and matches; Ted Moody's eight-point buck; and the open cupboard's wooden sides with pencil marks designating the climbing height of each new generation that makes us persist in keeping them? Why don't we give up the old porch swing, the rustic tin shower, the dented green canoe, or aluminum fishing boat and trade it all in for something more modern, efficient, and trendy?

Some might say we are overly sentimental, that we cling to a vanished era, that the cabin is a museum to the past. But I think not. There is a wonderful authenticity in being surrounded by living history, to know that those who loved and laughed before us shared the same simple joys and pleasures. Not only do we relish these treasured charms, but we also know from experience that it is all we want and need. By choice, our cabin remains the same. And that is exactly how we like it.

Consequently, by today's standards, Wake Robin appears humble.

No big-screen movies, high-speed Internet, video games, or DVDs fill its rooms. In fact, it was a big step to even add electricity in the 1950s.

Heading down to the lake for a swim on a hot day is a cherished and frequent activity.

In the early 1980s, we succumbed to further modernization by installing a telephone when a fourth generation was added to the roster. Hauling my three little boys 15 miles down the road to Dow's Corner Bar and Bait shop and then stuffing all of us into the roadside phone booth to call their dad working back home was the final straw.

A TV is not even an afterthought.

Regretfully, in the early 2000s we had to tear down our vintage log garage with its storeroom, guest sleeping area, icehouse/wood shed, long-ago outhouse, and two car stalls—a jack-of-all-trades buildings if there ever was one. It broke our hearts. Aging logs and lack of restoration funds were the culprits; a new log garage that blends with the cabin makes a fine replacement.

And so, Wake Robin's rustic simplicity continues.

For us, when the cabin's twig curtain rods are festooned with fragrant pine boughs and colorful wildflower bouquets grace its rooms; when coffee perks in the old tin pot and familiar aromas from the cast-iron skillet fill the cozy, sky-lit kitchen; and when a fire glows from the hearth and the kerosene lamps are lit, there is no place lovelier.

Perhaps Ben Mellinger, one of our father's lifelong college friends and a frequent visitor to the cabin summed it up best, "I've seen lots of places that are bigger and fancier, but no place more charming."

The fifth generation carries on the tradition of jumping through the cabin window onto porch beds.

To say we tend to agree is a vast understatement.

The lake, however, has changed. Similar-era log cabins have been torn down for bigger, more modern homes; screaming Jet Skis have replaced the sweet squeak of oarlocks; docks are no longer simple, green wooden affairs but wheeled metal contraptions side-saddled with awkward boat lifts; big-boat waves have eroded the islands' perimeters; and high-speed motors have usurped the puttering purr of small fishing boats leisurely crossing the lake.

Gone, too, are the once frequent moonlight howls of the wolves from the north wetlands of Big Spider; vanished are the rowboats full of fishing families anchored off the island points at dusk; no longer are docks bedecked with sunbathers or circled with swimmers.

And yet, for the most part, the lake and much of its wild, pristine beauty is thankfully still intact, allowing for the traditions we so love to continue. Although times have changed, what remains is a calming familiarity, the surround sounds of nature, and, for each of us, a strong sense of self.

By the time my three sons and their two cousins were born in the late 1970s and early 1980s, the Moody's Camp resort community as we knew it was long gone. No longer did square dances or lodge dinners offer an opportunity for lake friends, resort guests,

My granddaughter Elena about to enter my arms and Big Spider Lake.

and locals to gather. In the blink of an eye, a whole neighborhood's way of life dispersed.

A new era was in the making.

Despite the changes, all that we cherished and held dear was still there to pass on to the fourth generation, and so we eagerly introduced them to those joys. Perhaps most importantly, the experiences this fourth generation shared at the lake and cabin became a strong part of their childhoods and who they grew up to be: young adults with imaginations, intellectual curiosity, confidence, a love of nature, an appreciation of simplicity, and a strong spiritual connection to God's creation.

"It is certainly wonderful to be up here and all so very restful," wrote my father in 1940, after coming Up North with his mother from his job in Chicago. "No horns, streetcars or stoplights to worry about. . . . I had a wonderful sleep and feel so very rested today. I feel like a new person."

How true his words are for many of us today, seventy-two years later.

Of course, all has not been perfect.

It is not easy for multiple families to share a single cabin in the woods, no matter how much you love it or each other. Despite our best efforts, there have been hurts, disagreements, frustrations, differences, misunderstandings, and heartaches. And yet we have

Three sisters (left to right: Mary, me, and Nancy) on Picnic Island

persevered. Perhaps these personal challenges brought us to a deeper understanding of the complexities of each other's hearts.

For one of the main reasons that we continue to cherish this small cabin is that it is a reminder of the values we treasure: the joy and healing power of nature; the stewardship of God's natural world; the ability to share, compromise, and get along in a small space; the act of listening; the art of forgiving.

But mostly, why do we love it so?

Because of you, you dearly beloved family, you cherished friends. Your luminance, your light, your love, your laughter shone in this little corner of the earth, and, in the words of Robert Frost, that has made all the difference.

><

And now, beyond belief, members of a fifth generation are starting to dip their tiny toes into Big Spider Lake, lift their heads at a loon's call, look for eagles, and watch the pine needles swaying in the wind. Gratefully, my sons and daughters-in-law love the lake as much as we do and have chosen to carry on the traditions, while adding a few of their own, so that even my five little grandchildren have felt and sensed the joys. It didn't take long. Amazingly, four years ago, when Lily Clara—the namesake of her great-great grandmother—was just a tiny toddler, she greeted her grandfather Dave back home after a shared trip to the lake by immediately asking him, "Go to cabin?"

Already she remembered. Already the anticipation was there to go back to the place where there is no time, the place where—if only in our hearts—we are once more all together again.